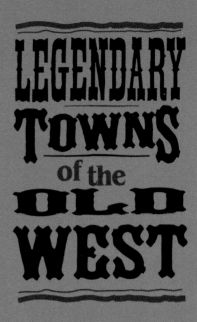

BUCKSKIN

An M & M Book

MALLARD
PRESS

An imprint of BDD Promotional Book Company, Inc.,
666 Fifth Avenue, New York York 10103

LEGENDARY TOWNS of the OLD WEST

Photographs by Lynn Radeka

TEXT BY JOHN BOWEN

MALLARD PRESS

An imprint of BDD Promotional Book Company, 666 Fifth Avenue, New York, New York 10103

Copyright 1990 by M & M Books

First published in the United States of America in 1990 by The Mallard Press.

All rights reserved.

ISBN 0-7924-5214-3

An M & M Book

Legendary Towns of the Old West was prepared and produced by M & M Books, 11 W.19th Street, New York, New York 10011.

Project Director & Editor Gary Fishgall; *Senior Editorial Assistant* Shirley Vierheller; *Editorial Assistants* David Blankenship, Ben McLaughlin, Maxine Dormer, Sarah Boyar; *Copy Editing* Burt N. Zelman and Vivian Maxfield Sansom of Publishers Workshop Inc.

Photo Research (Historic) Maxine Dormer, David Blankenship, Ben McLaughlin

Designer Binns & Lubin

Separations and Printing Regent Publishing Services Ltd.

(Preceding pages) 6th Street in Georgetown, Colorado

Contents

The settlement of the eastern United States was marked by civilization's steady advance inward from the Atlantic Ocean. By contrast, the West came into being in spasms, induced primarily by gold and silver strikes, and by the expansion of the cattle industry.

The Old West was the roughest, wildest, richest, and deadliest region America has ever known, peopled by freebooters, rascals, hell-for-leather cowboys, marauding Indians (who, in turn, were equally beset upon), and lonely prospectors. There were shady characters, including gamblers, con artists, prostitutes, and dance hall girls. There were also daring businessmen, mining magnates, and cattle barons. Even humble farmers went West, and, in the end, they survived all the others.

The frenzied search for fame and fortune by ambitious, even greedy, men and women created a wide open society where survival of the fittest was often the primary law. Towns were beehives of activity and violence was pervasive. In some instances, miners and cattle barons established their own kind of justice, which was often dispensed impulsively and imperfectly. Gradually, however, as a community settled into permanence, legally constituted authority replaced miner's courts and vigilantism.

The similarity of Old West towns was superficial. While most of them had one main street running through the heart of town, and it was lined with myriad buildings with false-front facades, each community had its own personality—and, in some cases, reputation. Some were primarily mining towns, others the haunts of cowboys and outlaws, and several were transportation hubs for the new and vitally important railroad.

Some of these places disappeared almost as quickly as they rose while others with similar ori-

City Hall in Tombstone, Arizona, built in 1882.

Introduction

gins continue to thrive to this day. Why the disparity? There is no simple answer; each community has its own story. County seats and state capitals—Sacramento, California, for example—had built-in economic bases that sustained them when the gold and silver dwindled and disappeared. Santa Fe, New Mexico, and Skagway, Alaska, enjoyed favorable geographic locations. Dodge City became a thriving agricultural center after the cattle drives ended. Towns that arose only for one reason—the presence of gold or silver—were at the greatest risk; prospectors and miners, loyal only to their lust for Eldorado, moved on when the wealth played out. But even some of these towns survived, either because the strikes were so great that commercial quantities of gold and silver persisted into the modern era, or because new uses for base metals, such as copper, kept them going. Some towns just hung on out of pure cussedness until a modern *raison d'etre*, such as tourism, could be found.

So popular is the Old West as a setting for movies and television shows that its taming has become the most romanticized part of American history. Is it still possible to separate fact from fancy? Can one still find the true aura of the frontier, and, if so, how can contemporary Americans experience it? These were among the questions in the minds of those who created this book. While a number of previous volumes had addressed these issues by examining the West's many ghost towns, none that we know of have done so by looking at the communities that *survived*. That, then, became our goal—to look for the lore of the Old West in ongoing, 20th-century towns. To identify the most likely prospects, state historical societies and tourism boards throughout the West were asked for recommendations. Photographers were contacted for advice on the picture potential of communities they knew. In the course of this research,

it soon became apparent that some states had a wealth of sites. In Colorado, Cripple Creek and Silverton-Durango could have certainly have been included in this volume along with the three towns that were selected. In other states—Texas being the most obvious one—a quintessential Old West town proved impossible to find. In the end, it was decided to limit the number of towns to 20 while covering the Western states as broadly as possible. As for Texas, Galveston was ultimately selected because of its premier role in the state's development, and because it brought a different aspect of 19th-century life to the book.

It would be virtually impossible to undertake a project such as this and not recognize the contributions of foundations, individuals, and local, state, and federal agencies, without whom the West would be a much duller place, at least visually. Their concerted efforts to preserve the architecture and artifacts of the past include the revival of communities that had declined drastically or been damaged by fire. In a few instances—Nevada City, Montana, among them—dedicated preservationists reconstructed a heritage that was almost totally destroyed by neglect and nature. Other towns—Virginia City, Nevada, and Tombstone, Arizona, to name two obvious examples—were brought back from oblivion by a combination of merchant zeal and historical enthusiasm. In some cases preservation is enshrined in law. New buildings in the old section of Santa Fe, for example, must conform to the traditional adobe style of architecture. Lincoln, New Mexico, where Billy the Kid gained much of his fame, is part of a ten-mile-long historical zone in which construction is controlled. Indeed, nowhere in the West is there a more dedi-

cated group of preservationists and town boosters than the Lincoln County Heritage Trust.

Community-sponsored interpretive programs help keep alive the period when miners and gunslingers jostled each other on narrow wooden sidewalks, stood shoulder to shoulder at bars that never closed, and settled their disputes in dusty streets with fists or guns. Dramas and annual celebrations re-create colorful historical incidents, such as the shooting of "Wild Bill" Hickok in Deadwood, South Dakota. Visitors today can rub elbows with reincarnations of pioneers like John Augustus Sutter, prospectors like Ed Schieffelin, gunslingers like "Doc" Holliday, cattle barons like John Chisum, and empire builders like Marcus Daly.

Distilling the essence of the Old West from bustling 20th-century towns took photographer Lynn Radeka of Garden Grove, California, on a five-month journey that covered more than 25,000 miles in 17 states. In Galveston, Texas, this student of famed naturalist-photographer Ansel Adams even saw history repeat itself when he arrived soon after a destructive hurricane (it was one such storm in 1900 that had deprived Galveston of its role as the leading city in Texas). He had his favorite sites—Butte, Montana, for example, because of the heavy emphasis on mining history—but at all of the 20 places in this book, he says "it seemed like I was alive in the past."

And that is the goal of this book as well—to give readers the feeling of being alive in the past. If one of the most telling ways of recapturing the Old West is to visit the very towns in which Western history occurred—the towns that have given rise to at least part of the legend—then hopefully this volume is the next best thing to being there.

The Great Plains and Rocky Mountains

DODGE CITY

KANSAS

This reconstructed facade of Front Street faithfully recalls the town's appearance during the 1870s. The buildings house a host of museum exhibits, some in re-created interiors, which are part of the Boot Hill Museum.

(*Opposite*) This statue of a steer stands for the five million Texas longhorns driven to Dodge City during the 1870s and 1880s. From there they were transported by rail to the slaughterhouses of Chicago.

(*Preceding pages*) The Bowman-White House in Georgetown, Colorado.

Dodge City's worst critic in its heyday was its own newspaper, which at different times described the boisterous cowtown as the "wickedest little city in America" and the "bibulous Babylon of the Frontier." The epithets were not unjust; on Front Street, frequented by gamblers, prostitutes, con men, skinners, soldiers, and cowhands, almost anything went. Legendary figures like Bill Tilghman, William Barclay "Bat" Masterson, and Wyatt Earp and numerous other gunmen whose names are unremembered are said to have sent a steady stream of victims, most of them guilty of some wrongdoing or another, to the Boot Hill Cemetery. When Kansas voted in prohibition in 1880, Dodge City paid little attention and remained noticeably "wet."

Until the middle of the 19th century, the site where Dodge City stands was an open plain where the Cheyenne and Kiowa Indians hunted antelope and elk, scalped adventurers bold enough to venture into their domain, and at times raided wagon trains moving along the Santa Fe Trail. In 1865, after repeated Indian attacks on transients, Fort Dodge was erected to protect travelers on the trail and to supply troops fighting Indians throughout the Southwest. The site of the fort was selected by Col. Grenville Dodge, who lent his name to the post.

The first construction on the site of Dodge City, some five

The Hardesty House, built in 1878, was moved to the site of the Boot Hill Museum in 1970. It was a cattleman's home in the late 19th-century.

The parlor of the restored Hardesty House.

The Editors

The man who published the local newspaper was an important member of the community. He was literate, articulate, and raised a powerful voice on matters affecting the town. It was not uncommon for the founders of a burgeoning community to advertise for, or solicit, a newspaperman from the East, rather than wait for one to arrive and set up shop. To be sure, the local editor - sought after or not - was expected boost town growth and development, helping to attract new settlers from wherever his paper might be read. As journalist Albert Richardson put it, a newspaper was "mother's milk to an infant town." Nathan Baker, publisher of the *Leader* in Cheyenne, Wyoming, for example, admitted that he gave less attention to local crimes than they deserved in order to preserve Cheyenne's image. He did, however, advise his readers to carry firearms at night.

Depending on the size of the community and the ambitions of the publisher, the paper might come out weekly or more frequently. The number of pages varied too. Some towns could even boast more than one newspaper. Leadville, Colorado, had three by 1880. Typically the front page was devoted to national news, picked up on a syndicated basis from larger towns back East and carried to subscribing papers by rail. Page two was often the opinion page. Thereafter would come the local news, a mix of serious stories and social tidbits. Advertisements, then as now, played an important role in financing a publication. Publishers not only sold the ads, they did everything else, with perhaps the assistance of family members or a young apprentice; they gathered the news, wrote the articles and editorials, laid out each edition, set the type, and ran the press. They often became printers for hire as well, running off brochures, broadsides, and other printed matter for local merchants and businessmen.

THE BOOT HILL MUSEUM PRINT SHOP

miles west of the fort, was a three-room sod house raised by rancher Henry L. Sitler in 1871. This single residence acted like a magnet, and soon numerous other simple houses dotted the grassy plain. The Dodge City Town Company was chartered in August 1872 to found a city on the Arkansas River at the 100th meridian, only a month before the arrival of the Atcheson, Topeka & Santa Fe Railroad. The early city, which took its name from the nearby fort, consisted of a dozen houses, a few adobe structures, and several dozen tents. Many of the first businesses were saloons.

At first, Dodge was known informally as "Buffalo City" in recognition of its role in the transshipment of the buffalo hides that hunters hauled in from the surrounding prairie. In all, about 2 million hides, a modest amount of buffalo meat, and 32 million pounds of bones, the latter used in making fertilizer, buttons, and other products, were shipped eastward before the nearby herds were depleted.

The cattle era began in 1876 when the first herds arrived off the Chisholm and Western Trails. It lasted only a decade, but it was the city's most prosperous and colorful era. Dodge became a sort of symbol of the gun-toting, hell-raising cow town of the Old West, an image that is invoked today by movies and TV shows. The image was never entirely accurate; the law-abiding people of Dodge City had their own

Cowboys shed their inhibitions when they arrived in Dodge City after a long drive, as this print by Frederic Remington illustrates.

Dodge City's Gunsmoke Street, formerly known as Walnut Street, was renamed in the 1960s to honor the long-running Western television series set in the fabled cowtown. The buildings seen here date from the early decades of the 20th-century.

shops, schools, churches, and neat houses, they enjoyed the prosperity brought on by the coming of the cattle drives but left the cowboys to celebrate trail's end without them.

Two of the West's most famous lawmen, Wyatt Earp as deputy marshall and "Bat" Masterson as sheriff, helped keep the peace during the time when Dodge City was reputed to be the toughest town in the West. Although Earp's exploits have since been so highly romanticized that it is difficult to separate fact from fiction, his reputation as a deadly gunfighter unquestionably was earned. And because of this reputation, or because of what his wife described as his "strange hold over men," Earp also possessed an uncanny ability to stare down violent men without bloodshed.

Before the cattle era ended in 1885, perhaps 10 million longhorns passed through the city on their way to the tables of Eastern consumers. They grazed in herds of 1,000 to 2,000 on the grass outside the town, fattening up after their arduous journey from Texas while awaiting the arrival of the eastbound trains that would carry them to the slaughterhouses of Chicago. As the railroads pushed closer and closer to the Texas ranches where the longhorns were bred, the long trek to Kansas became unnecessary, and Dodge City's role as a cow town ended. The city became an agricultural center for wheat and cattle. By the late 1880s, sheep ranching and farming extended for miles around.

A few relics of Dodge City's active past remain today, including some of the stone buildings erected in 1867 at Fort Dodge, which are now part of the Kansas Soldiers Home. One can also see deep "fossilized" ruts about 9 miles west of Dodge City, near Howell, which were created more than a century ago by thousands of wagons rolling west.

A "pharmacist" fills a "prescription" in the combination drug store and doctor's office at the Boot Hill Museum.

For the most part, however, the zesty flavor of the 1870s and 1880s is best recaptured at the Boot Hill Museum. Here, a combination of reconstructed and authentic buildings recall the days when cowhands gambled away and drank up the earnings of long, hard drives. The centerpiece of the complex is a reconstructed section of Front Street with facades of 15 connected establishments (the originals burned down in an 1885 fire). Behind the facades, a number of interiors depict common aspects of everyday life, including well-stocked general stores, a barber shop, an apothecary, saddle and gunsmith shops, a bank, and of course the Long Branch and other saloons.

Among the original structures relocated to the site are the two-cell jail built about 1865 at Fort Dodge, an 1882 windmill used to raise water on a prairie farm, and the 1878 Hardesty House.

The original site of Boot Hill Cemetery overlooks Front Street. A few simple grave markers have been erected to show how the cemetery looked when desperadoes were being buried there. A museum on the hill explores all aspects of Dodge City's history, from the world of the Indians before the coming of the whites to the lives of the cowboys and the importance of the railroad to the region. The Visitors Center is housed in the 1870s-style Great Western Hotel.

Operated by Boot Hill Museum, Inc., a nonprofit corporation, the complex stands a few blocks from Front Street, the original site. The first section of storefronts was completed in 1958, and others were added in 1964 and 1970. Old photographs were used to ensure authenticity of the reconstructions.

(*Opposite*) Boot Hill was the final resting place for many a gun-toting outlaw, and for numerous unknown fellows who helped tame the Wild West.

During Dodge City's heday, this well-appointed barber shop at the Boot Hill Museum would have been a lively gathering place for itinerant cowboys and townspeople.

Sheriff W. B. ("Bat") Masterson was among the famous lawmen whose quick guns preserved the peace in this boisterous cowtown.

DEADWOOD

SOUTH DAKOTA

Deadwood, virtually destroyed by fire in 1879, was rebuilt along the town's original lines and is today a National Historic Landmark.

(*Opposite*) The tombstone of "Wild Bill" Hickok in Mount Moriah Cemetery tells the story of the legendary gunfighter's untimely demise. "Calamity Jane" is buried nearby.

Gold had a rival in Deadwood—gambling! Indeed, Deadwood was so famous for its games of chance that sharps with their cards in their pockets and their roulette wheels in their wagons converged on the rugged and beautiful land from all over the West. Many high-living miners needed no coaxing to risk their hard-earned dust, but others were lured to honest and crooked games alike by smooth talkers who promised them a better-than-even chance of success. Only women dealers—regarded by miners as especially unscrupulous—found it tough going in Deadwood.

The man who became Deadwood's most famous citizen—as a result of his death—was attracted to the town by its reputation for gambling. His name was James Butler ("Wild Bill") Hickok. By the time gold was discovered on the Whitewood Creek at Deadwood in 1875, Hickok was already a Western legend owing largely to a flattering article in *Harper's Monthly* and the general belief that he had killed 35 men. But fame had hardly made him a wealthy man. Indeed, just prior to arriving in town, he had been unceremoniously kicked out of Cheyenne, Wyoming, for vagrancy. However, Hickok's reputation as the "prince of pistoleers" guaranteed his acceptance in the rough-and-ready milieu of Deadwood, and he eked out an existence at the gaming table.

Deadwood is located in a narrow gulch in the Black Hills of North Dakota. The beauty of the town's surroundings can be seen in this photo which features in the foreground the imposing spire of the old Deadwood Courthouse.

As a scout, lawman, and even a theatrical performer, James Butler ("Wild Bill") Hickok became one of the West's most celebrated figures. He was widely feared as a gunfighter, but devoted much of his time to gambling.

It came to a sudden end on August 2, 1876, while he was playing cards in Nuttal and Mann's Saloon No. 10. The day started strangely; Hickok, who usually insisted on sitting with his back to a wall so no one could sneak up behind him, was denied his preferred position by Charles Rich, one of the men in the game, but he played anyway. While Hickok concentrated on a hand of black aces and eights, Jack McCall, a former buffalo hunter, walked up behind him and shot him in the head. McCall's motives are uncertain—he later claimed that Hickok had killed his brother and had threatened him, which proved to be untrue; many believed he had been paid to kill "Wild Bill." McCall was tried and acquitted by a miners' court, which lacked legal standing, but was later convicted in a second trial and hanged in Yankton. Since the shooting of Hickok, aces and eights have been known as the "dead man's hand."

"Fearless Bill," as he was eulogized in a poem by Capt. Jack Crawford, is buried in Deadwood's Mount Moriah Cemetery. He was 48 years old at the

22

time of his death, according to his tombstone. Beside him, whether he would have wished it or not, lies "Calamity Jane" (Martha Jane Canary), who outlived Bill by 30 years. She claimed to have been secretly married to him, although he had a wife elsewhere, and insisted she be buried beside him in the hillside cemetery. "Calamity Jane's" talents as a scout were better than her reputation as a woman, but her unselfish act of nursing infected patients during a smallpox epidemic may have induced the town to honor her burial wish.

The story of Hickock and "Calamity Jane" is indicative of life in Deadwood, a latter-day Gomorrah, during the gold mining era. Murder and mayhem were common, but a crude form of justice and mercy prevailed. Perhaps in truth, Deadwood was no worse than any other gold camp, but from the start the town was bigger than life, known far and wide for its hell-raising atmosphere. Deadwood boasted that it had the prettiest women, the bravest men, and the "toniest bartenders" in the world. Whatever the qualities of its inhabitants, the town did indeed have 27 saloons and 14 gambling houses among the 166 businesses operating in 1876.

Deadwood was situated in the northern part of the Black Hills of South Dakota, sacred to the Sioux Indians and reserved to them by treaty. In 1874, Lt. Col. George Armstrong Custer led an expedition into the rugged forested wilderness and confirmed the widespread existence of gold in the region. Prospectors soon followed in Custer's wake. At first, the U.S. Cavalry tried to remove them, in keeping with its treaty obligations, but the task soon proved to be impossible. Most malefactors were released upon their promise not to return to the hills, a commitment most of them quickly broke. The treatment of one poacher who was scheduled to be prosecuted, Charles E. Solis, added to the legal complexity of the situation when the U.S. Attorney General decided that the treaty prohibitions

Custer and the Black Hills

GEORGE ARMSTRONG CUSTER

With his flowing golden curls, piercing blue eyes, and dashing uniform of his own design (with sailor-suit collar and scarlet cravat), George Armstrong Custer was a sight to behold. But he was not a popular fellow. Gen. David Stanley described him as "a coldblooded, untruthful and unprincipled man," and Capt. Frederick Benteen, who served under him, said, "I'm only too proud to say that I despised him." The son of an Ohio blacksmith, Custer attended West Point, graduating dead last in a class of 34, but distinguishing himself as a daring and resourceful cavalry officer during the Civil War. In 1866, he travelled West as lieutenant colonel of the newly formed 7th Cavalry. Seven years later, he and the 7th were directed to undertake a reconnaissance of the Black Hills in the Dakotas, land reserved by treaty to the Sioux. While the purpose of this mission was to establish a military outpost, Custer was also expected to confirm the presence of gold in the area, something which

prospectors had suspected for decades. He found little of the precious metal, but, perhaps to gain national attention, reported that gold was abundant. Soon hoards of miners were invading the territory. When the U.S. government sought to acquire the land from the Sioux, Red Cloud, their chief, demanded $600 million, a staggering sum. Instead of paying, the U.S. ordered the Indians to move within the designated reservation area. When those living off of the reservation, including the powerful Shaman Sitting Bull, refused, the government dispatched the cavalry, including Custer's unit, to force compliance. It was on this mission that Custer came to meet the forces of Sitting Bull at the Battle of Little Big Horn in June 1876. Within the space of an hour, he and his entire command of 215 men were wiped out. As it turned out, Custer's Last Stand proved to be the last stand of the native Americans too. Never again would they know such a victory.

Relics over the fireplace at No.10 Saloon include a pan, a pick, and period photographs.

The interior of No.10 Saloon looks much as it did when "Wild Bill" Hickok was shot in the back there while playing poker.

The architecture of many Old West gold rush towns features elaborate Victorian ornamentation, as this example in Deadwood illustrates.

against unauthorized entry did not apply to U.S. citizens. As additional gold strikes were made, the pressure mounted on the Cavalry to stop hindering and start protecting the miners.

The discovery at Deadwood in the autumn of 1875 was especially rich, and a flood of new miners swept into the hills. By spring, 25,000 hopefuls crowded into the town and the narrow gulch in which it sits. And thus the Las Vegas of the Black Hills was born.

Today's Deadwood conscientiously preserves its historical notoriety. Although a fire on September 26, 1879, destroyed much of the city and more

or less marked the end of the region's Gold Rush era, Main Street is being restored to a late-19th-century appearance and is a registered National Historic Landmark. Keno and craps tables, antique slot machines, carriages, and period clothing in the Old Days of Deadwood Museum provide insight into Deadwood's most notorious activity. In the Ghosts of Deadwood Gulch–Western Heritage Museum, wax villains, pioneers, prospectors, and Indians stare back at visitors. At the Broken Boot Gold Mine, a mile west of town, tourists may enter a shaft used by miners between 1878 and 1904. Another century-old tunnel illustrates

This 1880 Ansonia clock in the House of Roses illustrates the luxuries that gold brought to rip-roaring frontier towns

various aspects of the lives of numerous Chinese who were brought to Dead-wood in the 1870s to work on the rail-road and in the mines.

The murder of "Wild Bill" is recalled daily during the summer months at the reenactment of Jack McCall's trial. Also, a covered wagon is attacked once a year—in a bloodless way—by Indians, a not uncommon occurrence in Dead-wood's heyday.

Homestake Mine at nearby Lead, the largest gold mine in the Western Hemisphere, is still active. It has pro-cessed more than $1 billion in gold since its first lode was excavated in 1876.

A neon bucking horse is a modern addition to the Mint Bar, one of the oldest watering holes in the historic community of Sheridan, Wyoming.

(*Opposite*) This clock decorates one of the more than 30 historic structures that face Sheridan's Main Street, a thoroughfare that is on the National Register of Historic Places.

Choosing a town site on the basis of aesthetics was rare in the West during the 19th century, a period dominated by the practicalities of mass migration and the glitter of gold. Sheridan, Wyoming, however, owes its location to the beauty of its surroundings.

When John O. Loucks purchased a cabin on the future town site from Harry Mandel in 1882, he was familiar with the wide-open terrain where subtle variations of color streaked the Big Horn Mountains and the valleys. The rich soil and abundant water of the area, known to the Crow Indians as Absaraka, produced knee-deep grass and abundant wildlife, and the climate was mild. On a balmy May night in 1882, as he stood on a hill and watched the sun set, Loucks was inspired to sketch on a piece of brown wrapping paper the outline of a 40-acre town which would be named after Civil War Gen. Philip H. Sheridan.

There was little reason for Loucks to think that his town could become a reality. Not much had happened in the region since the arrival of the white man, probably in the 17th century. Jesuits visited the area in the 18th century; a map prepared by one of their number in 1792 accurately depicts the Big Horn Mountains. Explorers and a few settlers arrived in the early decades of the 19th century. A writer, Charles LaRaye, was

The Sheridan Inn, built by the Burlington Railroad and Sheridan Land Company, looks remarkably as it did when the imposing facility opened in 1893. The handsome bar, at right is one of the Inn's most attractive interior features.

among a group that passed by in 1802, for example. In 1807, John Colter took a side trip from the Lewis and Clark Expedition and was astonished by the natural phenomena of what is now Yellowstone Park. However, most of the westward-bound traffic followed the Overland Trail along the Platte River, through central Wyoming and into Idaho, leaving Louck's more northern territory to trappers and the Indians. Discovery of gold in Montana in the early 1860s brought a need for better access to the new mining communities, hence the opening of the Bozeman Trail, which ran north from Fort Laramie, Wyoming, through what is now Sheridan County, and then westward across Indian country to Butte, Montana. Army forts were established to protect an increasing number of settlers, merchants, prospectors, and

buffalo hunters, but early attempts to build a good wagon road had to be abandoned when even the U.S. Army could not provide sufficient protection from Indian raids. Martha Jane Canary earned her nickname, "Calamity Jane," by saving an Army captain during fighting near Sheridan.

Years of struggle between settlers and Indians elapsed, producing such bloody incidents as the Fetterman and Grattan massacres and the Wagon Box Fight, before Sheridan township was incorporated by the territorial legislature in 1884, with Loucks as mayor. The first cabin in the vicinity of present-day Sheridan apparently was built by two trappers on Little Goose Creek in 1878, only two years after the massacre of the 7th Cavalry at the Little Big Horn in Montana. In 1888, the town of Sheridan became the seat of

(Following pages) Sheridan's Old Train Depot preserves the flavor of the original station, and even features an antique train car, but inside one finds a collection of shops.

The Cattle Barons

WYOMING CATTLE BARON JOHN B. KENDRICK

In many parts of the West the first settlers were ranchers. Where land was inexpensive or free, they formed huge spreads comprising 100,000 acres or more. But, lacking a civilian or military authority, they had to defend their property themselves - against Indians, rustlers, and other ranchers. Indeed, disputes between spreads could turn very bloody. In Arizona's Pleasant Valley War, for instance, the conflict between the Grahams and the Tewksburys lasted five years and led to the death of between 25 and 50 people. By 1876, the railroad had reached Kansas, and station stops like Dodge City and Abeline became terminuses for massive cattle drives. Soon ranchers were wielding considerable power and influence. Many invested in the towns that grew up around them, creating hotels, stores, and newspapers. Some, like Wyoming's John Kendrick, became significant politi-

cal figures. Moreover, the allure of ranching attracted Eastern and European investors who hired experienced hands to manage spreads for them. But times were changing. The enormous herds had overgrazed much of the once-bountiful lands of the prairies and plains. The brutal winter of 1886/87 killed from 60 percent to 90 percent of some herds, and, when the thaw came, ranchers were so eager to sell their remaining stock that the market price for cattle plummeted. Many indebted ranchers had to sell parcels of their land to farmers. What was left was fenced in with the new-fangled barbed wire introduced by an Illinois farmer, Joseph F. Glidden. Then the railroad came to cattle country, making the long treks to the railhead obsolete. The golden age of ranching, which had lasted a mere 20 years (1866-1886), was at an end.

Martha Jane Cannary earned her nickname, "Calamity Jane," by saving an Army captain during a skirmish with Indians near Sheridan.

newly created Sheridan County; it remains so today. It was the area's rich, well-watered grasslands, ideal for ranching, that finally made Loucks's dream a reality. Well-heeled English cattle barons were among his early neighbors. The accidental discovery of coal in 1890, including the 34-foot bed at Monarch, created a new dynamism for the city. The Burlington Railroad arrived in 1892. Residential growth continued to escalate during the first three decades of the 20th century.

The hill at the southern end of Main Street provides a good overview of Sheridan's original 40-acre townsite. A walk along this thoroughfare, which was placed on the National Register of Historic Places in 1982, leads visitors past more than 30 historic buildings, many of them exhibiting mixed architectural influences, including cast-iron and false fronts. Three buildings near the northwest corner of Perkins Street, with their rounded balconies, turrets, and various porch styles, are a good illustration of Western eclecticism.

Among the other significant structures seen on an eight-block walk along Main Street are the Georgian Courthouse and Jail, built in 1905; 49 South Main, the only building in the historic area which is still a residence; the 1883 general store, the oldest structure in Sheridan; the 1923 Wyo Theatre, in Art Deco style; and several buildings

whose facades are prominently marked by a "K," to identify their association with John B. Kendrick, a pioneer rancher in the area as well as the state's governor and U.S. senator.

Sheridan Inn on Broadway, built by the Burlington Railroad and the Sheridan Land Company in 1892 and which at one time had the only telephone in Sheridan County, was saved from destruction in the mid-1960s by Mrs. Neltje Kings, an area rancher. It reopened in 1969 as a restaurant, meeting center, small museum, and art gallery.

Trail End Museum, once the home of Senator Kendrick, holds Western art, Indian arts and crafts, and military and pioneer artifacts, as well as some of the original Kendrick family furnish-

ings. The building was started in 1913 and completed in 1914.

The Bradford Brinton Memorial Ranch, 12 miles south of Sheridan, formerly the Quarter Circle A Ranch, is typical of the large turn-of-the-century cattle and horse spreads on which Sheridan's early wealth was built. Brinton, an Illinois native who purchased the ranch in 1923, also was a collector of Western art, and numerous paintings by Charles M. Russell, Frederic Remington, Edward Borein, George Bellows, John James Audubon, and others are on display in the 20-room ranch house. The family's antique furnishings, handmade quilts, silver, china, and other items remain. It was opened to the public in 1961.

The Bradford Brinton Memorial Ranch, 12 miles south of Sheridan, is typical of a large spread where cattle and horses were bred at the turn of the century.

GEORGETOWN

COLORADO

Most of the historic structures along 6th Street, the main thoroughfare of Georgetown, Colorado, have been restored. They are used for myriad business and civic purposes.

(*Opposite*) The Centennial House, whose style of architecture is often described as vernacular, dates from around 1870, and was constructed by David Nevin.

Near Georgetown, Colorado, there is an "Oh My God Road," a thoroughfare whose name pretty well captures the awe of the prospectors who came to the high valley previously visited only by mountain men and explorers. Surrounded by sharp, towering peaks, the area is rich in natural beauty, but the men had no time to appreciate their surroundings; locating and recovering gold was backbreaking work, even under favorable circumstances, and their new environment was tough and uncompromising.

But they were not disappointed by their findings. Starting in 1859 when George Jackson mistakenly thought the steam from hot springs was an Indian village, a succession of discoveries created gold camps with names like Idaho Springs and Silver Plume. The miners burrowed like moles into the hills and worked the streams—any place that looked promising as a source of gold. Among them were George and David Griffith, late of Kentucky, who moved upstream from the Jackson discovery into Upper Clear Creek Canyon. Their strike at the confluence of Clear and Leavenworth Creeks resulted in twin camps: George's Town, named after George Griffith, and Elizabethtown, named for his wife. When the communities later consolidated to become the county seat, the flip of a coin decided between the two names.

The Hotel de Paris was built in 1875 by a French immigrant named Louis Depuy. It was one of the finest establishments in the Colorado goldfields.

Louis Depuy squandered his inheritance in the Alençon region of France. Then he came to America, where he became the hotelier extraordinaire of the Colorado mining camps.

Georgetown was a goldfield anomaly from the start. Frontier life was rough and toughness was a virtue, but Georgetown was a gentler community than most. A heavy sprinkling of families arrived in the early stages of the town's existence to moderate the hell-raising atmosphere that usually pervaded gold camps. Consequently, Georgetown had almost as many churches as brothels, and half as many churches as saloons. The community also was fortunate in that it attracted men of culture and character, including

Louis Dupuy, an educated French immigrant who was determined to surround himself with comfort and refinement, and did so in his renowned hotel. Finally, the populace, which for a time was the third largest in Colorado, boasted a sense of community involvement and a degree of civic consciousness that was uncommon among the boom-and-bust communities of the West. Georgetown citizens took pride in their volunteer fire department, for example, which provided an essential service in an era when fires were an ever-present danger.

Such sensibilities, normally associated with permanent communities, were rare among gold towns, but they proved to be of considerable value to Georgetown, especially after the recovery of gold began to decline in the mid-

1860s. By that time, however, miners had determined that the mountains around Georgetown were laden with silver—the biggest vein to be found in the area until the great discovery at Leadville in 1878. Indeed, the Georgetown silver strike would yield approximately $200 million in the early years. The name of Silver Plume, now united with Georgetown in a single historic district and connected to it by a restored 1880s mining route, attests to the richness of the ore.

The silver bust of 1893 hit Georgetown and Silver Plume hard, but a small flow of gold continued to keep the town afloat into the early decades of the 20th century.

Georgetown's remarkable resiliency—as gold and silver mining communities went—has resulted in the preservation of more than 200 original buildings, many of them Victorian.

One of the finest buildings in the Colorado goldfields was the two-story Hôtel de Paris, and it remains the pride of Georgetown today, just as it was when Louis Dupuy presided over it in a grand manner. Built in 1875, the hotel and restaurant, which he described as "this little souvenir of Alençon," after his French birthplace, was famous throughout the Old West for its food and service. Dupuy took an interest in every aspect of the operation; for example, he was not only the owner but the supervising chef.

Entering the Hôtel de Paris, acquired in 1954 by the National Society of Colonial Dames of America in the State of Colorado, who continue to operate it as a museum, is like returning to a bygone era. The lobby, furnished with antique furniture, looks much as it did during its heyday. Dupuy's quarters

(*Following pages*) The fine furniture in the parlor of the three-story Hamill House depicts the lifestyle of a prosperous mine executive and civic leader, William A. Hamill, who built the home for his brother-in-law in 1867.

The Firefighters

The history of virtually every Old West town includes a succession of destructive fires. Consider, for example, Nevada City, California. The community went unscathed until 1852 when a fire erupted in the kitchen of the National Hotel, spread to the buildings on both sides and, in the end, destroyed 12 structures. Four years later, a blaze all but eliminated the town's business section, resulting in about $200,000 worth of damages. Another major fire broke out in May 1860 and yet another three months later and so forth. Like many other resolute Western towns, Nevada City simply rebuilt after each devastation.

TWO GEORGETOWN FIRE CHIEFS

THE EXTERIOR OF ALPINE HOSE NO.2, GEORGETOWN

The Board of Trustees did what it could to contain the danger by requiring each resident to provide a minium of four fire buckets and a vessel holding at least 50 gallons of water, but such laws could only help to an extent. Fires were endemic to frontier towns because buildings were usually constructed quickly, often with uncured, unpainted lumber which became more combustible as it dried, because structures were built very close to one another, often sharing walls, and because fireplaces often had no protective devices; some were even made of wood if stone weren't available. Given the risk of fire, the local volunteers who formed themselves into brigades were valued members of the community. Using ladders furnished at public expense, they paid for their own uniforms, and elected one of their own as chief. When reel hoses came along, they made the job a little easier. They also gave a brigade a means of testing its prowess against other companies. Such contests were fun and, at the same time, enabled firefighters to hone the skills of which they were justifiably proud.

retain his leather upholstered furniture and sizable library. The old-fashioned kitchen, where he personally oversaw the preparation of the food for which the hotel was famous, overlooks a courtyard. Upstairs bedrooms display large old-fashioned beds and washstands that provided an unusual degree of comfort for a frontier milieu. Other objects from the period include a large pendulum clock, Haviland china, diamond dust mirrors, and diverse paintings and etchings. The unusual staircase that divides at the top remains intact, as do the old wine cellar still stocked with the original barrels and the old brick furnace.

The three-story frame Hamill House is among the properties owned by the Georgetown Society, which is a leader in the restoration of the old mining town. The house gives visitors the feeling of stepping back in time as it reflects the life of a prosperous mine executive and civic leader, William A. Hamill and his family. Some of the furniture and artifacts are original to the house, including a red leather sofa and love seat and chairs. A small upstairs room has a stage where the children performed for the family. Hamill built the house for his brother-in-law in 1867, acquired it in 1874, and made several additions. Ancillary buildings include a two-room washhouse; a stone office building; and a carriage house.

Most of the original structures along 6th Street, the main thoroughfare, are restored for business and governmental purposes. These include several "blocks," or buildings housing multiple enterprises. Other historic structures include the Community Center, built in 1868 and used for more than a century as the court house; the Old Jail, a small stone building constructed in the 1860s; and several firehouses and churches.

The Georgetown Loop Historic Railroad has been restored in recent years for the enjoyment of visitors to the area. The Loop follows an 1880s mining route from Georgetown to the nearby town of Silver Plume.

Millions of dollars worth of gold and silver turned the one-time raucous tent city of Leadville, Colorado, into the solid, prosperous community that persists to this day.

(*Opposite*) Victorian decorative motifs enliven many of the homes in Leadville, including this brick residence on Harrison Avenue.

Leadville, Colorado, was a late bloomer in the mineral craze that enveloped the mountains of southwestern Colorado in the last half of the 19th century. Indeed, its development had been preceded by a number of exciting discoveries elsewhere in the California Gulch, that ore-rich region which got its name from prospector Abe Lee who announced his April 1860 gold discovery by shouting that he had "California in this here pan."

Lee and four partners were the first to discover placer gold in the inaccessible Arkansas Valley at an elevation of about 10,000 feet. The unpredictable, often harsh weather effectively restricted mining activities to six months of the year, and even then operations were hampered by large stones and heavy black sand. Despite the hardships, however, between 5,000 and 10,000 people were working every foot of land in the gulch by the end of 1860.

The gold boom yielded more than $5 million for its owners. But by the end of the Civil War, placer gold was becoming scarce, and prospectors began to look for riches elsewhere. Even the 1868 discovery of the Printer Boy lode—a large gold-bearing quartz deposit—did not halt the miners' exodus. Moreover, hydraulic mining begun in 1874 by William H. Stevens and Alvinus B. Wood was hampered by the black rocks

This home in Leadville features unpainted wooden siding and lace window curtains. Adorning the wooden porch are several cans which might have been used when the town was a boisterous mining camp.

and sand that had obstructed placer operations. Instead of tossing these impediments aside, Stevens and Wood had them assayed and discovered they contained 27 percent lead and 15 ounces of silver to the ton. They quietly consolidated numerous claims in the gulch and nearby hills before announcing their discovery. In 1877, Wood sold his share of the company to Levi Z. Leiter and left the region.

Leadville grew from that discovery. It was a raucous community where at first men occupied tents on eight-hour shifts and paid exorbitant prices for every kind of supplies. In 1877, George Albert Harris built a log hotel, and Charles Mater, a merchant from Granite, opened the first store. The well-worn path between these two establishments ultimately became Chestnut Street. The first house was raised in July 1877, with the Meyer Sampling Works and the Harrison Reduction Works following swiftly behind to service the new mines. The town then developed rapidly, hosting a population of between 20,000 and 30,000 during the boom years.

Additional Tabor influences can be seen in Leadville today. The three-story Tabor Opera House, built in 1879, recreates a slice of the fabulous silver-boom era, and today visitors may walk the stage where many of vaudeville's premier stars once performed. Its original painted backdrop, sets, and large curtain have been lovingly restored by a retired schoolteacher from Minnesota, Mrs. Florence Hollister, who purchased the historic building in 1955. Her descendants carry on the tours and the restoration program.

The frame Tabor Home was built about 1877 before Horace acquired his

H. A. W. Tabor was a Leadville storekeeper who made his fortune in mining. He was one of Colorado's wealthiest men before he lost his fortune in the 1890 silver bust.

The comfortable Tabor home, with its splendid Victorian furnishings, was built in about 1877, before H. A. W. Tabor acquired his fabulous wealth.

The Entertainers

The citizens of the bustling - and often - isolated communities of the West were starved for entertainment. Indeed, their love of the performing arts was so great that even the most celebrated figures of the day, including the great French actress Sarah Bernhardt, braved arduous travelling conditions to bask in their enthusiastic applause. Oscar Wilde included a number of Western towns in his 1882 lecture tour, and announced, in his inimitable style, that Colorado miners were the only well-dressed men he had seen in the United States. Edwin Booth, America's first great Shakespearean actor made exten-

LEADVILLE'S TABOR OPERA HOUSE

sive appearances on the frontier, reportedly earning as much as $25,000 a month. Shakespeare was quite popular out West. But melodramas, with such lurid titles as *The Widow's Victim* and *Ten Nights in a Bar Room*, were the mainstay of frontier theater. Variety shows also did very well. Featuring as many as 20 acts on a bill, these shows included singers, dancers, comics, and a host of novelty acts, such as magicians, acrobats, and trained animals. There were also minstrel shows - with performers appearing in blackface - and medicine shows, in which

sword swallowers, fortune tellers, and other unusual folk helped the patent medicine huckster sell his wares. One such troupe, the Big Sensation Medicine Company, had a cast of 31 and a tent that could hold up to 1,500 wide-eyed "pigeons." But the biggest draw of all was the circus. The mix of clowns, exotic animals, and aerialists decked out in brightly colored costumes, and accompanied by pulsing music stirred the hearts of townfolk everywhere. Even the toughest Western hombre could become a kid again - and did - when the circus came to town.

VAUDEVILLE PERFORMERS

fabulous wealth, and was moved to its present location on East 5th Street some two years later. In 1881, Tabor, who was then spending much of his time in Denver, sold the house to Melvin L. Clark, his brother-in-law. In 1952, after the home had been boarded up for many years, it was purchased by Mrs. Abbie D. Shannon, who restored it to its original condition. Presently furnished in the Victorian style, the home includes some pieces owned by the Tabors, which visitors can view on tours open to the public.

Other homes from the early mining era available for public viewing include the three-story Healy House, which served as a boarding house for teachers in the 1890s. Today it is owned by the state historical society, along with the log Dexter Cabin, relocated from

another section of town to Healy House grounds.

Among the two score or so other historic structures in Leadville are the *Herald Democrat* Newspaper Museum, a 1900-style newsroom that is still used to produce a newspaper; City Hall, built in the late 1880s as a post office; and the Leadville Colorado and Southern Railroad Company, which was reopened a few years ago to take passengers on a circuit that passes 19th-century relics and a molybdenum mine.

A multimedia show, *The Earth Runs Silver: Early Leadville*, in the historic Old Church next to the Chamber of Commerce on Harrison Street, provides an overview of Leadville's history. Additional mining lore can be found

at the Heritage Museum and Gallery, which is stocked with artifacts and dioramas on mines and miners, and the National Mining Hall of Fame and Museum.

The name of the camp, Leadville, was formally adopted at a meeting of the town's leading citizens on January 14, 1878. The first election of the newly incorporated city was held February 12 of that year.

The mines that opened on Fryer Hill in 1878 proved to be the richest in the region; in one 39-day period, the Robert E. Lee mine produced more than $250,000 in silver. At Leadville's peak in the 1880s and early 1890s, a dozen smelters were producing as much as $12 million in the precious metal per year. Like other mining communities, Leadville rode the roller-coaster course of boom and bust but, in 1895, two years after the bottom fell out of the silver market, the town's silver production for the year still totaled $7 million. All told, more than $2 billion in silver has been extracted from the area, and the precious metal is still being produced in the nearby Mosquito Range. Zinc and molybdenum were also mined, but they never rivaled gold or silver for the riches they produced.

The wealth of the region, particularly that on Fryer Hill, created fortunes which made their owners national celebrities. Among them were department store magnates Marshall Field and David May, and Meyer Guggenheim, who invested in the A.Y. and Minnie mines and founded a family dynasty based on smelting.

Leadville's favorite citizen of sudden wealth, then as now, was Horace A. W. Tabor, a storekeeper who sometimes grubstaked miners for a share of their findings. He made a good choice in April 1878 when he provided about $50 in supplies to August Rische and

A close-up of one of the homes on Harrison Avenue.

George Hook; their Little Plattsburg mine contained one of the richest silver deposits in Colorado, a 30-foot-thick vein. Tabor's one-third interest made him an instant millionaire. Subsequently, he acquired other properties which made him a multimillionaire. He became a town benefactor, and ultimately a U.S. senator before the silver bust in the 1890s dissipated his fortune. He then was named postmaster in Denver.

The Tabor story did not end so prosaically, however. During his wealthy period, Horace had divorced his first wife, Augusta, to marry Elizabeth McCourt Doe, better known as "Baby" Doe. Tabor never lost hope of a mining resurgence and, on his deathbed in 1899, he urged his wife to "hang on to the Matchless [mine], some day it will make millions." "Baby" Doe was faithful to his commission; she lived in penury on the property for 36 years, most of the time trying to work the mine alone. The mine site and cabin where she died in 1935 can be visited on a guided tour.

A horse-drawn surrey, which carries visitors on a tour of Leadville's historic sites, pauses in front of The Old Church.

TELLURIDE
COLORADO

Telluride's broad Main Street (now Colorado Avenue) is the heart of one of the nation's best preserved and most striking late 19th-century mining towns.

(*Opposite*) The San Miguel County Courthouse on Colorado Avenue. The building burned down shortly after it was completed in 1885, but the original bricks were saved and used two years later to build the present structure.

In Telluride, the south side of Main Street (officially Colorado Avenue, but almost never called that) is the cold side. In the winter, the sun passes along the ridge behind the buildings facing the street and its rays do not reach the sidewalk, which can remain frozen for months.

That meteorological fact could not be changed, of course, but it did not—and does not—inhibit activity on that side of the street. Indeed, the area south of Main Street was one of the hottest parts of town in the gold and silver mining era, with brothels (sometimes referred to as "ladies boarding houses"), gambling parlors, and saloons that could compete with those of any hell-raising town in the Old West. The area did not die out with the decline of mining either; some people living in Telluride today can remember when there were saloons and small "crib houses" where the "ladies" received their "guests," and when Prohibition made bootlegging a prosperous business.

Telluride owes its founding to the discovery of a rich combination of silver, gold, lead, zinc, copper, and iron in 1875 by prospector John Fallon. Subsequent discoveries created an instant mining boom. One of the mine owners, J. B. Ingram, got his start by discovering that the Union and Sheridan claims exceeded the legal limits and claiming their excess property. Appropriately, his mine was given the exotic name Smugglers.

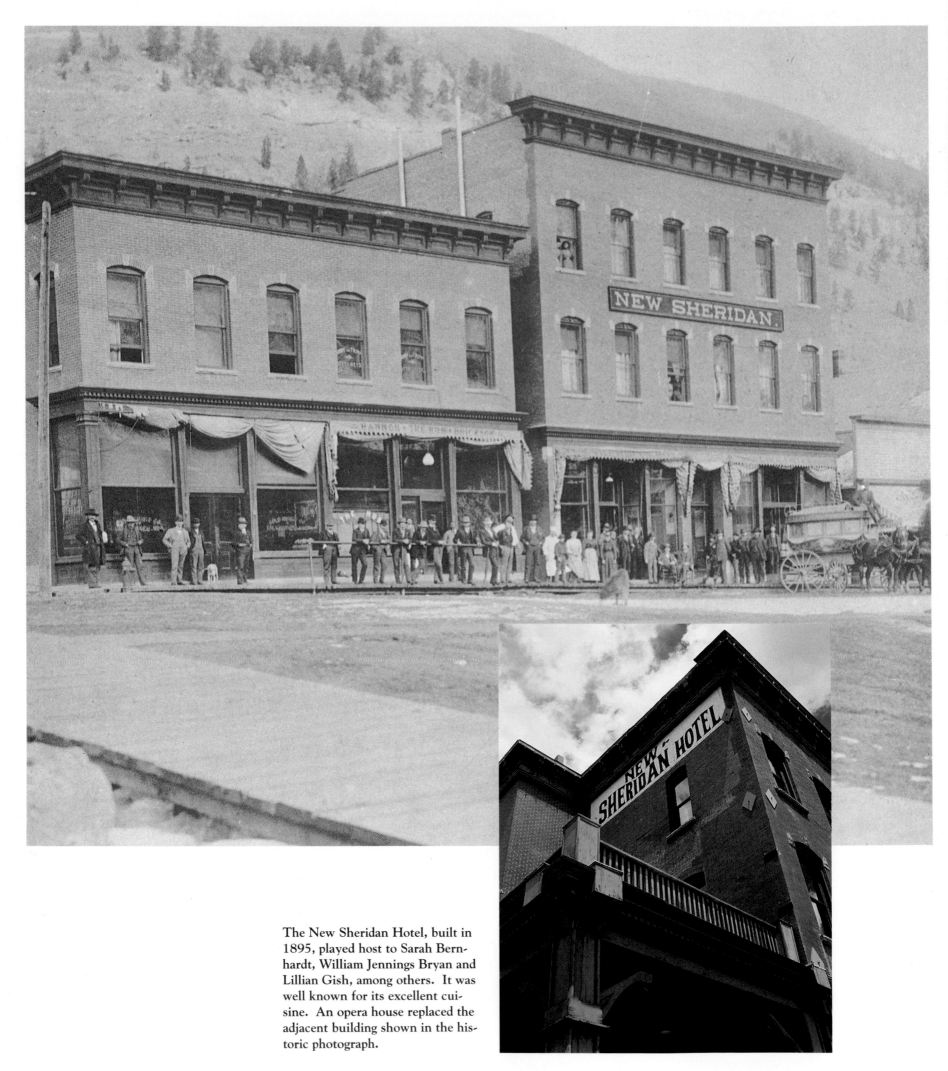

The New Sheridan Hotel, built in 1895, played host to Sarah Bernhardt, William Jennings Bryan and Lillian Gish, among others. It was well known for its excellent cuisine. An opera house replaced the adjacent building shown in the historic photograph.

The rich ore on the claim produced 18 ounces of gold and 600 ounces of silver per ton. Ultimately, consolidation reunited the properties in the Smuggler–Union mine, which in the decades prior to 1900 dug more than 35 miles of tunnel into the hills around Telluride. The mine continued to produce into the modern era, and is still maintained by the mining company.

Among the other rich mines were the Tomboy, Pandora, Argentine, and Liberty Bell. The Tomboy strike, which occurred in Savage Basin some 3,000 feet above Telluride, was so productive that the Rothschilds of London purchased it in 1897 for $2 million. Both the Liberty Bell and the Pandora constructed ore-processing mills, which shipped millions in bullion to the U.S. Mint in Denver.

The 8,700-foot altitude of Telluride combined with the inaccessibility of the ore in the nearby peaks to demand a special brand of ingenuity from the miners. Mule trains labored up steep, narrow roads built into the sides of the peaks. Aerial tramways, one 6,700 feet long, were constructed to carry miners and supplies to the shafts dug into the hillsides. Materials for buildings constructed on ledges above sheer cliffs were hauled up piece by piece and assembled. The unusual width of Telluride's Main Street, which is immediately apparent to visitors, was created to provide turnaround room for mule teams carrying long lengths of cables, coiled in succession on frames that were tied to the mules' backs. An enlarged photograph of several such mule teams turning on the street hangs on the wall of a shop adjacent to the Visitors Center.

Silver was king for almost two decades, drawing a population of 3,000 by 1890. The demonetization of silver in 1893 brought hard times, and the population of Telluride shrank. However, the town's role as county seat provided a degree of stability and permanence. Although small amounts of gold were recovered from mine dumps, the local depression lasted about five years, until

Fine wood paneling, wall sconces, and floral wall decorations reflect the opulence of the New Sheridan Bar during the era when Telluride was a bustling mining town.

Links to the World

As people began to populate the West, they hungered for news of home. Just as importantly, events were taking place on the frontier - such as the discovery of gold in California - that were of interest to the people back East. To facilitate communication between the coasts, Congress created an overland mail service in 1857, reducing by more than 50 percent the time that it took to carry a letter from St. Louis to San Francisco (from about two months to about three weeks). Then came the celebrated Pony Express, which offered ten-day service from St. Joseph, Missouri, to San Francisco. Wiry lads of 18 years or younger galloped all the way, changing mounts every 12 to 15 miles (it took 75 horses for the entire journey). It was difficult and dangerous work, but the Pony Express riders were among the West's most celebrated heroes. Then, in October 1861, the service became obsolete - the transconti-nental telegraph had been completed. Still, it took years for telegraph wires to cover the vast expanse of the frontier. In 1876 there were only 3,000 miles of line in the entire nation; by 1900 there were 1.4 million. Businessmen used the new technology to a greater degree than the average citizen - the wealthiest even maintained ticker tapes in their offices so they could follow fluctuations in the stock market - but the average person could - and did - send telegrams as the occasion warranted. A more personal form of communication arrived with the advent of the telephone. As with the telegraph, it took time for the new technology to make a difference in the lives of the average Westerner, but, by as early as the mid-1880s, switchboards were cropping up here and there. The terrible isolation borne by so many frontier families had come to an end.

gold was discovered in commercially feasible quantities. The recovery of the community was short-lived, however; strikes by the miners, which produced bitterness and violence, crippled an already shaky industry. The heyday of the precious metals era was over, but the mines continued to produce base metals in large quantities until the 1970s.

An attempt in 1938 to make Telluride a ski resort was aborted by World War II. After that, the town was by its own admission a "dying community" until Joe Zoline, an entrepreneur from Beverly Hills, California, decided in 1968 to turn the nearby hills into a winter recreation area.

The influx of vacationers has inspired Telluride, one of the best-preserved and most striking mining towns in Colorado and a National Historic Landmark since 1963, to rediscover its historic roots. For example, it has reinstituted the tradition of waking the community for the annual Fourth of July celebration with a dynamite explosion—apparently required in the late 19th century to arouse all-night revelers, though fewer people now need such a loud wake-up call.

Main Street has an extraordinary assortment of handsome late-19th-century buildings on both sides of the street, most of them housing businesses

Except for the installation of modern equipment, this handsome bar in the New Sheridan Hotel looks much as it did when thirsty 19th-century miners bellied up.

(Opposite) Mining the rugged peaks above Telluride required aerial tramways, one of which was 6,700 feet long. These vehicles transported miners and supplies to the hillside shafts.

of various types. Among them are the 1895 three-story brick New Sheridan Hotel, where presidential candidate William Jennings Bryan gave an often-repeated version of his famous "Cross of Gold" speech; the 1883 Old Drug Store, whose current occupant, a real estate firm, displays an old-fashioned marble counter, patent medicines, and other relics; and the Roma Bar, one of the town's oldest, with a handsome carved walnut bar constructed in 1860 that is an attraction in itself.

Also on the street is a plaque marking the site of the bank where one of the West's legendary outlaws, Butch Cassidy, reputedly made his first heist (the building later burned). The "Galloping Goose," beside the court house, was an unusual vehicle made of train and automobile parts that operated on the rail line into Telluride.

A walking tour mapped by the Chamber of Commerce also includes more than a dozen structures along Pacific, Columbia, and Galena Avenues and crossing streets. In the southern end of town, relics of the red-light district known in the 1880s and 1890s as "Popcorn Alley" include the Silverbell and Senate saloons and several "crib houses" (now small, individual homes). A few blocks away are the homes and meeting halls of Finn Town, where many of the Scandinavians settled.

The town's leaders lived north of Main Street, and the area is still pretty much intact. The Old Waggoner House on the corner of Pine Street and Galena Avenue is not the town's oldest, but it is the one that many inhabitants of Telluride revere most. It was the home of Charles Waggoner, president of the Bank of Telluride, who outsmarted New York bankers in the 1929 crash and preserved the savings of his depositors. Sent to prison for swindling the Eastern financiers, he was released after three years but never returned to Telluride. Nearby structures include the L. L. Nunn House, home of the man who built the world's first high-voltage alternating current power plant; the 1883 Town Hall, first used as a school; and St. Patrick's Roman Catholic Church, built in 1895.

At the top of Pine Street is an imposing brick structure built in 1895 as a hospital; it now houses the San Miguel County Museum. Inside, one room is devoted to gambling history. Among the other displays are a turn-of-the-century dentist's office; a complete barber shop; mining scales and other equipment; scores of old photographs; and antique children's toys.

Three-time Democratic party standard-bearer William Jennings Bryan is shown here in around 1896 when he ran for U.S. president for the first time. During the campaign, he gave one of his stirring orations from a platform of Telluride's New Sheridan Hotel.

Nevada City has been revived by the restoration of about eight original buildings and the relocation of about 100 structures from other places in Montana.

(*Opposite*) Virginia City's old buildings, including many frame structures dating back to the 1860s, have been masterfully restored.

(*Preceding pages*) Nevada City, Montana.

In the Old West, a prospector finding traces of gold immediately faced a critical question: how much was there? Such was the situation on May 26, 1863, when Bill Fairweather and one of his partners, Henry Edgar, checked an outcrop hoping to find enough gold to buy some tobacco when they got to town. While Edgar washed small piles of dirt, Fairweather poked at bedrock with a knife. Fairweather found "a scad" but Edgar found even more in the wash, enough to convince all who heard about it that Alder Gulch was a rich find.

Within a few days, the forested trails into the rocky gulch were crowded. The first group to arrive quickly set up a crude form of government and named their community Varina, for the wife of Confederate President Jefferson Davis. That appellation was quickly rejected by a Unionist judge, who, in a compromise with the Southerners, selected the name Virginia City. Other boom towns followed, including Nevada City in 1863; within a year, 10,000 people lived within 20 miles of the strike.

Virginia City had a special kind of lawlessness, much of it organized by Sheriff Henry Plummer of Bannack, another mining town about 70 miles away. His road agents, popularly known as "innocents" after their password, "I am innocent," robbed hundreds of miners and stagecoaches, and committed

Wells Fargo

LEGENDARY WELLS FARGO DRIVER WILLIAM H. ("SHOTGUN") TAYLOR

California's tremendous population boom in the late 1840s created significant business opportunities. Two New York businessmen with the vision - and the means - to take advantage of them were Henry Wells and William G. Fargo. Their Wells Fargo & Co., founded in 1852, gave miners a badly needed way of converting their diggings into currency and provided other banking services as well. By 1854, Wells Fargo was the third largest bank in the state; when the financial panic of February 1855 ruined larger enterprises, it met the demands of its depositors and kept on growing. In time its many branch offices in California and Oregon came to include banking houses in New York, British Columbia, Nevada, and Utah as well. Meanwhile, the company also pursued a thriving shipping business. It was instrumental in the establishment of the Overland Mail Company in 1858, and took the helm of that endeavor two years later, inaugurating a shipping service between Sacramento and Omaha, Nebraska. Using Concord Coaches, which Mark Twain called "a cradle on wheels," Wells Fargo promised to make the journey of 1,900 miles in 15 days. It averaged five miles an hour, changing horses every 12 miles, and made rest stops (with meal service) every 45 miles. Like other carriers, Wells Fargo became an attractive target for outlaws. One, known as "Black Bart," robbed 27 coaches between 1875 and 1883. Eventually, he was found to be a respectable mine engineer named Charles Boles, and was convicted of his crimes. The company continues to thrive to this day, but its express service ended in 1918 when the federal government ordered the consolidation of competing carriers as a wartime measure. With its passing, another bit of the Old West faded into history.

VIRGINIA CITY'S RE-CREATED WELLS FARGO OFFICE

more than a hundred killings before justice caught up with them. Law and order was restored when the disgusted citizens of Virginia City formed a vigilante committee, on or about December 20, 1863, hanging 32 outlaws during the next four months. They often printed pointed notices in the local newspaper warning that "the ends of justice shall be carried out." On one occasion, five men were simultaneously hanged on the corner of Wallace and Van Buren Streets. Sheriff Plummer's criminal career came to an abrupt end when he was arrested January 10, 1864, in Bannack. He was hanged, ironically, on gallows he himself had commissioned. (Some of the graves of the road agents hanged by the vigilantes can be seen today in Boot Hill Cemetery.)

The Virginia City Players perform 19th-century plays, including melodramas, in the manner of a period touring company at the stone Virginia City Opera House, built about 1898 as Smith and Boyd's livery stable and renovated in 1949 for its present purpose.

Nevada City, which deteriorated as a ghost town for many years, has been revived by the restoration of about eight original buildings and the relocation of about 100 structures from many different places in Montana. Original buildings include the Don L. Byam House, built in the 1860s by the judge of the miners' court which tried George Ives for murder (the crime that resulted in the creation of the vigilantes).

One section of the town recalls the contribution of Chinese immigrants to the mining history of the state. About 2,000 Chinese lived in the gulch during the boom years. The houses, cabins, laundry, general stores, and other buildings reflecting this Asian-American heritage are grouped around a replica of a temple which stood in Nevada City during the mining era.

Visitors may experience some of the atmosphere of the Old West in a number of other ways. They may pan for gold, listen to the tinny tunes of numerous old mechanical music

This stagecoach at Nevada City carried one of the many itinerant photographers who were drawn to the excitement and beauty of the West. It is possible that the vehicle belonged to Carleton Watkins, a noted photographer of the period who is known to have visited Butte.

(*Following pages*) The ample stock of Virginia City's Buford store included packaged food, bulk coffee, tea, seeds, baking soda, and soap.

An old cycle hanging on Wallace Street becomes a piece of folk sculpture. The bicycle craze which began in the 1890s post-dated the period when miners tugged balking mules along the town's dirt streets.

machines at the Nevada City Music Hall, or stay at places of accommodation designed to re-create the era. Two of the rooms in the Nevada City Hotel (built during the late 1950s in frontier style) are furnished with Victorian antiques such as ornate four-poster beds, velveted chairs, and a pump organ. Its cabins are authentic miners huts which have been restored and modernized, and its two-story outhouse is a popular place for picture taking. At the frame Fairweather Inn, patrons may sit on the old-fashioned porch and balcony and look out on a town scene reminiscent of that witnessed by many a sourdough. The lobby of the inn is furnished in Victorian antiques.

Meanwhile, the stream of bullion flowing from Montana caught the attention of President Abraham Lincoln in Washington, D.C., who on May 26, 1864—exactly one year after the discovery of gold—signed a bill creating

The *Montana Post*, which occupied this unpretentious building in Virginia City, was the state's first newspaper.

(Opposite) Children learned the three Rs in one-room schoolhouses like this one at Nevada City. Montana's first public school was in Virginia City.

the Territory of Montana. Bannack was the first capital, but the seat of territorial government was moved to Virginia City on February 6, 1865, and remained there for 10 years. Virginia City was also the location of the state's first public school and the headquarters for many of the professional people and organizations which served Montana during its formative years.

But more than anything, it was gold that kept Virginia City growing. In the first three years alone, $30 million worth of ore was removed from the earth. Even today gold and silver continue to contribute to the local economy, while talc mining is still going strong in nearby valleys.

Virginia City and Nevada City, only little more than a mile apart, relate the story of Montana's greatest gold strike in different ways. While they are twin cities, they are not identical twins. Virginia City is an original; Nevada City is largely a re-creation. The narrow-gauge Alder Gulch Short Line Steam Railroad, which connects the two, displays vintage railroad cars.

Virginia City's old buildings, including many frame structures dating back to the 1860s, have been masterfully restored since the early 1940s, primarily under the guidance of millionaire rancher Charles Bovey and his wife, Sue. Wooden sidewalks and dirt streets connect 25 restored buildings which are furnished as an assay office, Montana's first newspaper office, a grocery store with 19th-century goods, clothing and jewelry outlets, a Wells Fargo office, the Bale of Hay saloon, and other common goldfield businesses.

Henry Edgar and his partners found gold in Alder Gulch and started the rush that created Virginia City.

The Thompson–Hickman Memorial Library and Museum and the J. Spencer Watkins Museum emphasize Old West history, especially the region's mining past and ranching heritage. The old territorial administrative center is still standing. Known locally as Content Corner because it was built in 1864 to house the clothing store of Solomon P. Content, it has held various tenants in recent years.

71

The Berkeley Pit Mine dominates the east slope of Butte Hill, often described as the "richest hill on earth."

(*Opposite*) Balanced geometric patterns in grey and white stone add to the charm of the Curtis Music Hall, built in 1892. The style is described as Victorian eclectic.

Like comedian Rodney Dangerfield, "the richest hill on earth" got no respect at first. When gold was discovered in the early 1860s on Silver Bow Creek by two Virginia City prospectors, G. O. Humphreys and William Allison, the overflow of argonauts naturally extended northward to Butte Hill. The creation of the town of Butte on the gentle slope was almost an afterthought; gold was never found there in large quantities.

Butte remained just another town until 1874, when William L. Farlin filed claims on quartz outcroppings which he had quietly assayed and found to be very rich in copper, silver, and gold. When word of the silver lode got around, Butte became a boom town full of boisterous miners and unscrupulous exploiters. Within a year, the population rose to 4,000. Silver sustained the high life for the remainder of the decade, but Butte had yet to reach its peak.

It wasn't the glitter of gold or the shine of silver that proved to be Butte's Mother Lode. It was copper, a base metal actually discovered in the area in 1866 by Joseph Ramsdell and largely ignored until 1875, when Michael Hickey, a Union veteran of the Civil War, staked out the Anaconda claim near the Alice and the Moulton silver mines. The timing was right; the modern era was beginning to stir, especially as a result of

Employees of the Butte Water Company are hard at work in this black and white photo taken in around 1900. The attractive facade of this building can be seen in the color photograph of Granite Street.

Thomas Edison's experiments with electricity, which gave rise to a host of industrial and household appliances and, in turn, created a ready market for the baser metals. By this time, the concept of consolidating mines was also well-established. In Butte, individual claims were never prevalent, however, because copper didn't offer prospectors the romantic allure of gold or silver.

The men who developed the mines, the copper kings, were a patient but vibrant group, full of ideas and plans. Even the toughest, most experienced of them were convinced that "nowhere else has . . . the hidden forces of nature contrived to concentrate the wealth," as one of their number put it. They formed financial consortia, issued notes and stock, and created conglomerates, the kind of detail that bored sourdoughs but created empires. Some of the great names of American finance, including William Randolph Hearst, vied for control of The Hill, and the steady flow of rich ore it produced. Subsequent decades witnessed bitter legal and political battles among those who wished to be king of The Hill. Especially noteworthy was the dispute between Marcus Daly, who had arrived in Butte as a teen-age immigrant and rose to head the Anaconda Copper Company, and W. A. Clark, a rival mining magnate. Clark wanted to see the relocation of the state capital to Helena, and in that he was successful, but in the end Daly's Anaconda Copper Company emerged as the sole mine owner of the "richest hill on earth."

Subsequently, thousands of miles of tunnels were dug, some descending nearly a mile into the earth. Copper extraction reached a peak in the 1920s, and not until the 1950s did the supply of high-grade ores come to an end and the open pit mining of lower grade ores begin. Thereafter, the east slope of Butte Hill became the Berkeley Pit, an open hole where ore was moved by truck along the tiered cuts in the hill.

The ornate interior of the Butte-Silver Bow City-County Courthouse, built in 1910-12.

The Miners Bank Building, once a department store, was reconstructed after the original structure was destroyed by fire in 1905.

The expansion of the pit, visible from the Visitors Center on Park Street East, required relocation of whole sections of the city's population from time to time.

Butte Hill has yielded more than 20 billion pounds of copper. Although the industry was somewhat depressed in the 1970s and 1980s, copper mining is still an important economic force in the community.

Butte has been as malleable as the metal that has underpinned its economy. More than 60 ethnic groups have migrated to the mining town to work in the mines or establish businesses. Advancement was unlimited for those who could master the technical complexities and the physical and emotional demands of mining. It was not unusual for a one-time water boy like Cornelius F. Kelley to rise to the presidency of Anaconda Copper Company.

High rollers are usually high livers, and those in Butte were no exception. They imposed an indelible imprint on the city that is readily visible today. They built mansions, financed the first electric main-line railroad, enacted *Ben Hur* with live horses on stage, bounced prohibitionist Carry Nation out of a

Butte's World Museum of Mining and Hellroarin' Gulch, where visitors walk the streets of simulated mining camps.

A Copper King and his Mansion

The son of a Pennsylvania farmer, William Andrews Clark (1839-1925) went West, like so many others, to seek his fortune, but, unlike most, he found it. Starting as a peddler in the goldfields of Colorado, he entered the wholesale business, then went into banking and mining. He also acquired control of several newspapers in Montana and Utah, giant sugar plantations and rich oil-bearing land in California, and extensive real-estate holdings. He created the first water company in Butte, Montana, the first electric light company, and one of the first trolley car companies. In 1884, he decided to create a mansion befitting his station as one of the nation's wealthiest men. Three years later, the three-story, 30-room home designed in the Renaissance revival style by Los Angeles architect C. H. Brown was completed. It cost approximately $280,000 at a time when Clark's estimated earnings came to $17 million a month! European craftsmen handcarved woodwork throughout the house and frescoed the ceiling of every room of the first two floors. The mansion boasted a 62-foot-long ballroom, stained glass windows by Louis Comfort Tiffany, fixtures fitted for incandescent lighting as well as gas, and an impressive main staircase with intricately carved panels of birds and flowers from various countries of the world. The latter, called "The Staircase of Nations," was temporarily removed from the house in 1903 and exhibited at the St. Louis World's Fair. Eventually, when Clark became a U.S. Senator, he erected a 121-room mansion in New York City. That structure was torn down, at his request, upon his death, but his home in Butte survived. The oldest mansion in Montana, it is privately owned by Mrs. Ann Cote Smith, who lovingly restored the home with her mother, Mrs. Anna Cote, and is open to the public.

THE EXTERIOR (top), BEDROOM (above), AND INTERIOR DECOR (right), OF THE COPPER KING MANSION

W. A. Clarke, a mining magnate whose success as a politician resulted in his appointment to the United States Senate.

The Copper King Mansion, a 32-room Victorian-Elizabethan home located only two blocks from the arts center, is open to visitation. Built in 1888 by William A. Clark, its fine woodwork, Tiffany windows, and antique furniture illustrate how the copper monarchs lived.

Other historic structures within a few blocks of the arts center—most of them still used as residences and businesses—include the home of Butte's first mayor, Henry Jacobs, built in the late 1870s; the 1884 Connell Home, the oldest surviving mansion; the Butte–Silver Bow City-County Courthouse, built from 1910 to 1912, which features the capstan of the battleship U.S.S. *Maine*, a stained glass dome, and murals; St. Patrick's Church, the oldest Roman Catholic house of worship in Butte; and the 1904 B'nai Israel Synagogue, the oldest functioning synagogue in Montana. The turn-of-the-century Old Butte Fire Hall, now the public archives, has an extensive collection of old newspapers, photographs, family records, and other documents.

The life of a miner can be lived vicariously in a number of ways. Visitors may pan for gold; walk the streets of a simulated mining camp at the World Museum of Mining and Hellroarin' Gulch; ride a period train from the site of the old Orphan Girl Mine to the Kelley Mine; and view the town aboard Old No. 1, an early open streetcar. The museum of the Montana College of Mineral Science and Technology exhibits the rocks on which the community's fortunes were built, as well as other minerals and fossils.

A rival of Clarke, Marcus Daly was adept at the rough and tumble competition among the copper magnates. He emerged as "King of the Hill" in Butte.

bar, held a dance attended by 400 men and 4 women, and became the first to play keno. The old section of the city was declared a National Historic Landmark in 1962.

A self-guided walking tour starts at the Charles Clark Mansion. This copy of a French château, built for the son of the copper king, is now the community arts center, displaying original paintings by Western artist Charles M. Russell and others. The 18-block tour passes 40 sites dating from the late 19th century, 19 of which are within five blocks of the starting point.

Main Street in Idaho City, with the courthouse in the foreground.

(*Opposite*) The Idaho *World*, the state's oldest operating newspaper, was founded in 1863. It moved into this building four years later.

In 1862, the peaceful, sylvan nature of the Boise Basin, in which Idaho City is located, contrasted sharply with most of the country. The Civil War raged from Virginia to Kansas and even far-away California was unnerved by rumors of Confederate raids.

Idaho's peace and isolation ended suddenly in August, not because of the war, but because gold was discovered on the Boston Bar near Centreville. The controversial death of one member of the 12-man party that discovered the shiny flecks was a harbinger of things to come.

It was obvious to all newcomers that the bounteous natural beauty of the Boise Basin hid great fortunes. Almost every rushing stream that lapped at rocks in the forests contained gold, the lodestar of the 19th century. The area also was isolated and could be reached only by an arduous overland journey. Distance and deprivation did not discourage the confirmed argonauts of the age, however. Prospectors traveled singly on foot or horseback, in small parties, and in mule pack trains that stretched out for hundreds of yards. Indeed, enterprising businessmen found a way to cash in on the strike before reaching the goldfields; they operated a pack mule ferry service which for $50.00 transported a passenger and a small amount of baggage from Umatilla, Oregon, on the Columbia River to

Placerville, Idaho Territory.

Many experienced sourdoughs from California and Oregon hastened to Idaho and lent their expertise not only to mining but to organizing and staffing the towns that quickly sprang up in the region. Right behind the prospectors came the inevitable merchants, gamblers, confidence men, petty thieves, highwaymen, lawyers, doctors, prostitutes, clergymen, and actors. Less than a year after the discovery, about 16,000 people lived in the basin. In 1864, wagon roads and a stage coach route from Umatilla made the goldfields more accessible.

The town that soon became the largest, Idaho City, was not the first. Its origins date to October 1862, when a few of the boys from the site now occupied by Centreville checked out an area between Grimes's and Elk Creeks. The results of their digging were so impressive that they returned to their camp in a flush of excitement. They tried to keep their find a secret from all but their closest friends, claiming that their agitation came from being chased by a bear. It didn't work. Soon, an army of men were working claims staked out along Elk and Mores Creeks and around Gold Hill. Almost overnight, Idaho City became the largest town in Idaho Territory; within three years, it was the largest city in the Northwest, replacing Portland, Oregon. More than 200 businesses lined Montgomery and nearby streets, including saloons, a brewery, the Jenny Lind Theater, bowling alleys, music stores, clothing and general stores, and even bakeries. In 1866, Idaho City's population was estimated at 5,800, despite a disastrous fire in 1865 which

St. Joseph's, established in 1863, was one of the first Roman Catholic churches in the state.

The Lawmen

Hollywood liked to portray them as stalwart champions of justice. Bat Masterson called them ordinary men "who could shoot straight and had the most utter courage and perfect nerve - and, for the most part, a keen sense of right and wrong." But neither Hollywood nor Masterson caught the true measure of the law enforcement officer, for more often than not he was a shady character, one who was closer in spirit to the outlaws he was sworn to apprehend than he was to the citizenry in his care. The townfolk didn't really mind if he had been an outlaw before he became a marshal, or if he invested in saloons or brothels as a sideline as long as he could keep the peace. In areas rife with troublemakers - notably the cowtowns and mining towns - such a pragmatic attitude was perhaps understandable. But, even in the most raucous of communities, gun battles and fistfights were not what occupied the major part of a marshal's time. He spent a good portion of each day doing paperwork. He issued licenses to brothels and saloons, served as the sanitation inspector, and collected taxes (taking a share of the proceeds for himself). Even "Wild Bill" Hickcok, the marshal of Abeline, Kansas, had to keep the streets litter free and patrol for unlicensed dogs. But the local marshal wasn't alone; he was part of a network of frontier law enforcement officers that also included county sheriffs and, in a few states, quasi-military outfits, like the Texas Rangers. At the pinnacle of this network was the U.S. marshal, appointed by the president to oversee a state or territory. These were political figures. In Colorado, for example, a wholesale liquor dealer was a federal marshal, as was a bank appraiser. Fellows like these usually left the earthier aspects of the job to their deputies.

BOISE COUNTY SHERIFF JOHN LEARY IN HIS OFFICE

Boise Basin Mercantile, near the center of the historic district, is Idaho's oldest existing store. The building was constructed in 1865.

destroyed 80 percent of the buildings. Other fires in 1867, 1868, and 1871 devastated the community, but each time the city was rebuilt.

The beautiful surroundings of Idaho City did not temper the character of those who came to the goldfields. The number of saloons dispensing whisky far exceeded the number of places offering cultural diversion. The revelry often spilled out onto the streets. Tempers were short, and life was cheap; gunfights arose frequently over perceived slights, idle boasts, or sundry other disputes.

The Boise Basin was extremely rich in gold—more than $250 million in bullion was extracted in a few years—but the vein was a flash in the pan. Within a few years, its volume of mineral wealth dropped drastically, and the exodus of miners began. Those who remained turned to dredging operations in 1898, but the population continued to decline until the total reached a low of 104 in 1920.

While Idaho City's attention today is focused partly on outdoor activities, including skiing in nearby areas, the community does not ignore its colorful

Hoses like this one in the Idaho City firehouse were essential in fighting the flames that plagued mining towns throughout the West.

The Miner's Exchange Saloon
opened in 1865 after discoveries
on Gold Hill made Idaho City the
largest community in the Northwest.

past. It is carefully preserving a historic area where structures from the early 1860s stand beside those rebuilt after each of the fires, creating an interesting juxtaposition of architectural styles representing several different decades. The flavor of the Gold Rush era also is maintained in a variety of small ways: the wooden sidewalks, the graffiti carved by prisoners on the log walls of the Old Jail, the headboards in Pioneer Cemetery, and the Gold Rush relics displayed in the Boise Basin Museum.

Many of the 15 sites listed on a walking tour stand in a four-block area along Montgomery and Main Streets, with the 1865 Boise Mercantile, Idaho's oldest existing store, near the center. Other key structures include the 1867 Idaho World Building, seat of the state's oldest operating newspaper; the log Idaho Penitentiary built in 1864; the 1860s Galbraith and Kenn Smith Houses, good examples of mining camp residences; and the Pon Yan House, owned by a prosperous Chinese businessman who was among the thousands of Orientals who participated in the Idaho City Gold Rush.

A short distance off this main area are St. Joseph's Roman Catholic Church, established in 1863, and the Odd Fellows Hall, built in 1875 and the oldest such meeting house in Idaho.

The ongoing restoration of Idaho City is to be fostered by a revolving loan fund, which would assist individuals interested in the historic preservation program.

Built in 1891, this handsome frame structure served as a schoolhouse for 70 years. It is now the city hall of Idaho City.

California Street in Jacksonville, Oregon, is the heart of an historic district that preserves more than 80 original brick and frame buildings, many from the gold rush period.

(*Opposite*) Bovine heads on the side wall of this old brick structure advertise the products of a dairy established in Jacksonville in 1888. The window was obviously cut later.

O regon conjures up a lot of images: forest greenery, salmon runs, the port of Portland, an active, solid population with a sense of history. But most people do not usually associate gold with the Beaver State. Yet, Oregon was a Gold Rush site, whose streams and valleys yielded sizable quantities of the precious metal.

No place typifies this oft-forgotten role better than Jacksonville in southwest Oregon, where in 1851 two mulepackers working their way from Portland to Yreka camped for the night at Rich Gulch and discovered gold.

In many respects, the history of Jacksonville is typical of gold boom towns throughout the West. It roared into existence and quickly became the largest town in southern Oregon. In the whole state, it was surpassed only by Portland, which offered a favorable jumping off point for the gold finds in the coastal and north central states. Jacksonville had all the faults of the typical Western gold town—it was brassy, raucous, violent. It also had many of the virtues of such communities—it settled what formerly was a wilderness area, attracted a virile and innovative population, and helped fuel the economic expansion of the United States.

As the largest community in the region, Jacksonville was by default the center of government. It officially became the

county seat in 1853 and soon began imposing a limited kind of order on the rugged individualists attracted to goldfields. But the town was beset by many of the challenges that destroyed other communities. Shortages of staples were common; at times, salt was literally worth its weight in gold. An 1868 smallpox epidemic killed many of the inhabitants, including some of Jacksonville's leaders, who were among the first settlers. Then, a flood inundated the town with tons of rock and mud, and fires caused extensive damage. The Takelma Indians, who inhabited the area before the whites arrived, resisted encroachment on their traditional lands, especially after treaties were broken. Bloodshed ended when members of the tribe were captured and marched north to a site near Newport.

But despite these obstacles, the production of gold saw Jacksonville through the hard times. Solid multi-story commercial buildings rose along the main streets during the 1850s, near the stately homes of community leaders. At the time, Jacksonville was the most important community between San Francisco and Portland, with a population estimated at 15,000.

Then, as the 1860s opened, the in-

The appearance of California Street hasn't changed very much since the early photograph was taken in 1884.

Jeremiah Nunan, a prominent merchant, ordered the plans for this handsome mansion from an Eastern catalog. It was built in around 1890.

The Prospectors

They were sailors and shopkeepers, clerks and soldiers, dreamers from every walk of life, who dropped what they were doing with the news of a strike to pursue their luck in the gold- and silverfields of the West. They came in droves. Indeed, it is estimated that 80,000 fortune-seekers made the journey to California in 1849 alone. Most of them could barely afford a pick, a pan, a mule, and some food. Consequently, the methods that they used for finding gold were rather unsophisticated. The most popular approach called for the use of a pan with a porous bottom - or a rocker or cradle - with which a prospector could sift a streambed, washing away the sediment with water while the heavier ore remained behind. Most worked long and hard in this fashion with little to show for their effort; they would have earned more per hour had they stuck with their old jobs. Some drifted from strike to strike for years in search of the Mother Lode. Others gave up and returned home or forged new lives in the West. There were also those who came to the goldfields and built fortunes by supplying the prospectors with badly needed goods and services. Among them was a German immigrant who came to San Francisco with a large supply of canvas which he planned to sell to the miners for tents. When he arrived in the goldfields, however, he found that they needed pants more than shelter, because panning for gold in the rugged terrain had worn out their trousers at the knees. So he used his canvas to make pants, switching to denim when his material ran out. His name was Levi Strauss. And the pants he developed? They became a world-wide phenomenon called blue jeans.

PROSPECTORS NORTH OF JACSONVILLE, CIRCA 1895

evitable occurred. The take of gold dust from the waterways dwindled, and the miners began drifting to more promising sites. Jacksonville stayed afloat for a time as the seat of Jackson County and the trading center for the farmers of the fertile Rogue River Valley. But the Oregon and California Railroad bypassed the town in favor of Medford in 1884, and it lost much of its farm trade. Then, the county seat was relocated to Medford in 1927. That marked the end for Jacksonville's elevated stature, and the population dropped to 1,500. But the town managed to hang on; it never became a ghost town, as did many smaller communities in the region.

The permanent residents of Jacksonville initiated a comeback in 1950 by restoring the 1883 courthouse as a museum exhibiting pioneer and Indian relics, photographs, and railroad history. Since then, more than 80 original brick and frame buildings spanning the formative years of the town's life have been restored. Almost half of the buildings, scattered through an area of more than 25 blocks, survive from Jacksonville's heyday in the 1870s and 1880s. The old town is a National Historic Landmark.

Many of the historic structures, such as the 1891 Rogue River Railroad Sta-

(Opposite) The Beekman House, built in 1875, retains its original furnishings. Guides in 19th-century costumes conduct tours of the residence.

tion housing the Chamber of Commerce Information Center, retain their external charm and historical authenticity while serving contemporary business needs. Small shops and four bed and breakfast establishments are among the ongoing concerns that occupy historic structures.

A few buildings are open to the public as museums. The 1863 Beekman Bank, which also was an express office, retains all of its original furnishings, including the gold scales and Wells

Fargo posters. While most of the residences are still private, the house built by gold freighter and banker C. C. Beekman in 1875 can be visited during the warm months.

The United States Hotel was built in 1880 by George Holt to fulfill a promise to his fiancée. Among the first guests was President Rutherford B. Hayes.

The oldest surviving brick structure in town, the 1855 Brunner Building, is on Oregon Street. Nearby buildings include an 1861 store, which in the mid 1860s became the town's first post office; and the 1855 J. W. McCully Building, whose upper floor was a meeting room in the 1850s when the lower floor housed a general merchandise store. Among other significant buildings are the 1854 Methodist Episcopal Church, the oldest religious struc-

The Beekman Bank, which opened in 1863, retains original furnishings, including the gold scales that converted pokes and nuggets into cash.

Cornelius C. Beekman, who left a strong imprint on Jacksonville, made his fortune in the dangerous trade of transporting gold from mines to depositories.

ture south of the Willamette Valley; the 1861 Eagle Brewery Saloon, which remained in operation until the early 1900s; and the Old Jail, which now houses the hands-on Children's Museum depicting the life of Indians and settlers.

The impressive First Presbyterian Church, which dates from 1881, has stained glass windows shipped from Italy via Cape Horn.

SKAGWAY
ALASKA

The Red Onion Saloon, at the far left, was built in the early 1900s. It is one of more than 30 historic buildings on Broadway, Skagway's main thoroughfare.

(*Opposite*) A gold dome identifies the Golden North Hotel, built in the early 1900s. It continues to operate as a hotel today.

Explorers and trappers had reported glitter in streambeds as early as 1867, but the first rich Alaskan strike occurred in 1880 when Fred Harris and Joe Juneau discovered gold in Silverbow Basin, near what is now the capital of the state. That was a respectable strike by any standard; more than $150 million in gold was recovered.

But in the big one, the Klondike Gold Rush of 1896, the object of desire was not even in Alaska. Droves of argonauts hustled northward in response to news of the discovery of flaky gold "like cheese in a sandwich" at Forty-mile Creek in the Yukon Territory. Many who believed they were heading for Alaskan goldfields found themselves facing an arduous journey over high mountain passes to reach Canada's gold-bearing streams.

The name given to the Gold Rush—Klondike—was a corruption of the Indian word *Thron-Diuck*, or Hammer-Water. It was universally accepted by the prospectors, whether they actually worked the Klondike River and its six tributaries or some other stream in Alaska or Canada. The name meant gold, and plenty of it.

The mass movement that followed—involving prospectors from many lands—left unforgettable photographs of heavily burdened men struggling in a chain to climb the snow-covered

Jefferson Randolph ("Soapy") Smith (center) masterminded a gang of con artists and cut throats, but he posed as a businessman and philanthropist.

A "soft sculpture" artist in historic Skagway has given life to his own Klondiker complete with a pan full of gold nuggets.

The reception desk of the Golden North Hotel.

(Opposite) During the era of the Klondike gold rush, household items such as these in the Trail of '98 Museum had to be shipped from Seattle, Washington or Portland, Oregon. At the time, Alaska was largely a barren, unsettled frontier.

Chilkoot or White Passes into the forbidding interior of northwestern Canada.

They had arrived by steamer—from Seattle, Washington; Vancouver, British Columbia; Portland, Oregon; and San Francisco, California—to disembark at the head of Lynn Canal, northern terminus of Alaska's inland waterways.

To service this influx, the town of Skagway soon sprawled along the waterfront where Capt. William Moore and his family had once peacefully farmed. As soon as steamers began discharging prospectors, Moore's farm was occupied by squatters—a "nest of ants," in the words of one observer—who threw up a tent-and-shack town. Within a few months, the population exceeded 10,000, making it the largest town in Alaska. Moore protested to the local government, but instead of recognizing his property rights, the town ordered him to move his home because it blocked the route of a planned street.

Skagway was a prime example of the rowdy West at its most chaotic. It was "little better than hell on earth," according to one Northwest Mountie whose job it was to try to keep the peace at the Canadian goldfields. During the warm months, ship after ship landed fresh contingents of prospectors there. Many newcomers lost their precious supplies to thieves and were unable to move on because Canada required a minimum stock to enter its territory. Others arrived with dreams of gold and little idea of either the logistics involved or the sacrifices required. When they realized what confronted them, they waited to take the next boat south. Many more stayed than left,

The Eskimos

A TOTEM POLE, SKAGWAY

For the most part, they didn't huddle in ice-block *igloos*, as the stereotype would have it. Rather, the Eskimos lived in semi-subterranean dwellings of driftwood and sod. While these houses were small - 14 feet on average - they often boasted trim wood planks on the floor and walls. There were wooden sleeping platforms as well, and sometimes even cupboards. Long entrance tunnels, which were lower than the rest of the structure, kept the cold out of the main dwelling, and seal oil or wood fires kept things toasty. Eskimos lived in permanent villages, averaging between 12 and 100 people. The focal point of each community was the *kazgi*, or ceremonial house, where the men worked and social events were held. When the Europeans discovered Alaska in 1741, the Eskimos shared the land with two other indigenous groups, the Aleuts, and the Indians (made up of Tlingits, Haidas, and Athabascans). The three groups, of which the Eskimos were the largest, had different languages and customs, but they shared a similar way of life. They were hunters and gatherers; in the case of the Eskimos, who were primarily a coastal people, marine animals (especially seals) were the principal prey. They all used the waterways for traffic; their boats, or *kayaks*, made of driftwood or whalebone and stretched sealskin, were masterpieces of construction - light weight, balanced, and durable. They didn't engage in agriculture, nor did they raise domestic animals (except dogs). They believed in a supreme being and an afterlife, and honored the spirits in food and animals. The shaman - part priest and part doctor - was a powerful member of the tribe. When the Europeans arrived, there were roughly 23,000 - 35,000 Eskimos living in Alaska. There were 34,144, according to the 1980 census. But no longer were they the largest group in the land. Whites, lured to Alaska by gold, and later, by oil, out-numbered them by better than 9 to 1.

A DOOR MURAL, SKAGWAY

The locomotive of the White Pass
Railroad gets up steam.

The depot of the White Pass and
Yukon Route Railroad was built
in 1899 to transport travellers
between Skagway and Whitehorse. The depot is now the Visitors Center of the Klondike Gold
Rush National Park.

however, and the outfitting, portage, and guide businesses boomed. So did those catering to more primal needs; four saloons were among the first businesses to rise in the new town, as were gambling halls and brothels. Conditions got so bad that U.S. Army troops were sent there in 1898 to maintain order.

Amid the chaotic conditions, one entrepreneur who thrived was Jefferson Randolph ("Soapy") Smith, who organized a gang of con artists and cutthroats to prey on newcomers and prospectors with bulging pokes. Posturing as a businessman and philanthropist, he saw that his victims had fare to return to Seattle, shared a platform with the governor of Alaska, and raised a unit to serve in the Spanish-American War (which the U.S. government refused to enroll). He was shot to death July 8, 1898, in an altercation while trying to enter a meeting of vigilantes aroused by his depredations. The next day, the known members of his gang were arrested and deported. "Soapy" and his opponent in the gunfight, Frank Reid, are buried in the Gold Rush Cemetery.

Unlike "Soapy," Mollie Walsh was a tragic figure. The petite girl, who had bravely ventured alone to Alaska, had natural charm. She won the heart of many a rough prospector and packer. In a gunfight, Jack Newman, an ardent admirer, killed a gambler who had told him to stay away from Mollie, but in the end she married Mike Barrett, a packer, and they moved to Seattle. There, she deserted her husband and left town. When she returned, he shot her. Newman never lost his love for Mollie; he had a memorial to her "inspiring spirit" erected in Skagway. The act of remembrance got him into trouble with Hanna, his wife, and he had to place his memorial in Seattle.

The careers of "Soapy" and Mollie are just two of the colorful tales invoked by the Skagway Historic District. Here the Gold Rush era is re-created by wooden sidewalks, historic buildings, horse-drawn carriage rides, the Trail of '98 Museum, a slide presentation in the Visitors Center, and a reenactment in the Eagles Hall entitled *Skagway in the Days of '98 with Soapy Smith*. The hall also features dance hall girls, gambling with play money, and other reminders of those turbulent Gold Rush days.

Structures on Broadway Street look much as they did during the closing years of the 19th century, when the street was teeming with prospectors, when merchants were busy outfitting them, and mule-skinners plodded along with supplies to sustain the miners during the long, harsh winters of the interior. More than 30 historic structures front the street, including nine which are part of the Klondike Gold Rush National Historical Park.

The White Pass and Yukon Route Railroad Depot, which houses the park's Visitors Center, was built in 1898 to serve a line connecting Skagway to Whitehorse, Yukon Territory. It features exhibits on the Gold Rush era, conducts an active interpretive program, and is the starting point for walking tours of historic Skagway. Other historic structures in the national park include the Martin Itjen House, built in 1901 by one of the town's greatest post-gold era promoters; a tailor's shop; a dry goods store; a bakery; and several saloons.

An additional score of structures stands nearby, including four owned by the National Park Service, which administers the park.

Like most goldfield towns, Skagway's fortunes fell almost as quickly as they had blossomed. When the flow of gold diminished, the exodus began, and the town shriveled to 600 people. It's renaissance began after World War I when it became a historic attraction for visiting cruise ships.

The scramble to the Klondike in 1896 was followed by gold discoveries in Nome, Alaska, in 1899, and Fairbanks, Alaska, in 1902—the last of the great "rushes" in a period distinguished by its extraordinary lust for gold. It may well be the last of such adventures in history; it is unlikely that this kind of an event could occur in the modern world, where there is so little unclaimed space.

Fraternal organizations thrived in most mining towns. One founded by Klondikers was the Arctic Brotherhood Lodge No. 1, which used this hall, constructed in 1899.

The "inspiring figure" of Mollie Walsh softened the hearts of the rough and raucous prospectors who visited her grub tent during the gold rush period.

GALVESTON

TEXAS

The charms of the Victorian age permeate Galveston's waterfront area known as the Strand, where historic buildings now serve as shops and restaurants.

(*Opposite*) The Bishop's Palace, constructed in 1886, has been designated one of the 100 best designed buildings in the United States by the American Institute of Architects.

(*Preceding pages*) The Montaño store in Lincoln, New Mexico.

At a time when Indians roamed the West Texas frontier and drovers herded cattle up the Chisholm Trail, Galveston was an established and sophisticated city with a large, civic-minded population. Texas's first national bank was opened there, as was its first post office, naval base, medical college, hospital, opera house, and public library. Galvestonians were the first Texans to possess the steam locomotive, the telephone, electric lights, and the electric street car. Despite rapid developments elsewhere in Texas, it remained, throughout the 19th century, the state's largest city, the banking and commercial capital, and the principal seaport. It was, simply put, the state's most important city.

This eminence came to a sudden end in 1900, when a hurricane swept across the city's island home leaving death and destruction in its wake. At least 6,000 people were killed and whole sections of the city were carried away or wrecked. Galveston, which had shown a resilient spirit on numerous earlier occasions, never fully recovered. Bankers and businesses simply moved to Houston—hot and humid but relatively safe and already developing into a metropolis.

Being a runner-up was a new role for Galveston, but it adjusted with the grace of a grande dame. By 1902, it had begun to revive and to devise means of avoiding such

destruction in the future. To prevent, or at least limit, future hurricane damage, it shored up the foundations of buildings, elevated many from 3 to 17 feet, and built the "great wall" of Texas, a 17-foot-high, 10.4-mile-long barrier against the ravages of nature. This seawall stabilized the long curving beachfront, where people sunbathe and fish with nets. Along Seawall Boulevard are numerous motels, restaurants, shops, and museums.

Galveston's earlier history is just as spotty as its weather, and somewhat obscure. The Karankawa Indians were the first to paddle to the island in some dim historical past, but left few lasting remnants of their presence. Spanish ships stopped at the island as early as the 16th century, but it was named in the 18th century for Bernardo de Gálvez, Spanish governor of Louisiana and later viceroy of New Spain. In 1814, the pirate Jean Lafitte selected it as a hideout and named it Campeche (usually spelled Campeachy). From here, he sallied forth on profitable raids against Spanish ships until the United States forced him to cease and desist in 1821. He burned Campeachy before departing but left legends of buried treasure on the island that persist to this day.

Galveston's rush to the top of Texas communities began in the days of the Lone Star Republic, when the town was selected as the first naval base and served in 1836 as temporary capital. It was already Texas's largest seaport and principal financial center by the outbreak of the Civil War and, during that conflict, was a principal site of Confederate military activity. It also was used by ships running the Union blockade of the Confederate coastline. After the war, Galveston continued to grow and prosper and soon found itself the state's premier city.

When the bishop of the Galveston-Houston diocese is in residence at the Bishop's Palace, he can look directly across the street at Sacred Heart Roman Catholic Church from this porch.

Pirate Jean Lafitte used Galveston Island, which he called Campeachy, to prey on Spanish shipping in the Gulf of Mexico.

This corner of the Stewart Building shows the extensive ornamentation that appealed to Texans during the Victorian age.

A Relic from the Age of Sail

During the 19th century the Tall Ships were the masters of the world's oceans, bringing exotic cargoes to their ports of call from the far corners of the earth. Such a ship was the *Elissa*, a three-masted barque with an iron hull built in 1877 in Aberdeen, Scotland, by Alexander Hall & Company. Her owner was Henry Fowler Watt of Liverpool, who named her for his niece. She was an impressive sight but, even before her maiden voyage, *Elissa* was a bit of a dinosaur. Steam power was rapidly making sailing ships obsolete. Still, she proudly flew the British flag for 20 years until she was sold in 1897 to a Norwegian company and renamed *Fjeld*. In time she would be sold again, to Sweden where she became *Gustav*. Finally, she wound up as the *Christopheros*, a motorized smuggler in Greece. By the 1970s, she was a rusting hulk, scheduled

THE RIGGING (above) AND INTERIOR (below left) OF THE *ELLISA*

for salvage. Then a marine archaeologist, Peter Throckmorton, recognized a 19th-century sailing ship beneath her often-modified and dilapidated surface. Hearing of the discovery, and perhaps remembering the *Elissa*'s visits to Texas in her heyday, the Galveston Historical Foundation agreed to purchase the barque and bring her to the Lone Star State. Her decks were rotting, she had no masts, and no sails. There weren't even any plans showing her construction, for they had been destroyed during World War II. Still the Texans plunged in. It took two years but, using Oregon trees for masts, and a deck of Douglas fir caulked with oakum, they worked their magic. On July 4, 1982, the *Elissa*, looking once again like a 19th-century master of the seas, opened to the public as a maritime museum in her permanent birth in the Port of Galveston. Two months later, she took to the seas again. Today she regularly navigates the waters of the Gulf of Mexico guided by a crew of 50-70 volunteers. The Age of Sail was a glorious part of America's history and now it lives on in Texas.

Much of the charm of modern Galveston had its origins in the 1890s, when author Stephen Crane waxed poetically about the "thousand details of street color and life." This splendor, most evident in the historic area of the city, is emphasized by more than 60 varieties of oleander in beautiful parks, wide beaches, quaint waterfront structures, and traditional bath houses. Despite nature's destructive assaults, Galveston boasts more than 1,500 historic structures, 550 of which are on the National Register of Historic Places.

The Strand, the restored waterfront area between 20th and 25th and Water and Mechanics Streets, has an excellent concentration of Victorian iron-front buildings, accented by gaslights. These handsome structures now house art galleries, speciality and antique shops, hotels, bed and breakfasts, restaurants, pubs, an old-fashioned candy factory, and the Center Theater, where a 12-minute movie explores *Galveston: Island of Discovery*. The Strand is alive with pedestrians, horse-drawn carriages, and trolleys during the warm months. Annual events include "Dickens on the Strand" the first weekend in December, during which characters from Charles Dickens's novels and late-19th-century "Bobbies" intermingle with carolers, jugglers, mimes, magicians, bell ringers, tightrope walkers, and other street performers. Mardi Gras is observed in February, and a Homes Tour is held the first two weekends in May.

The homes which are open to the public illustrate the diversity that has characterized Galveston's history. One of the oldest is the 1839 Williams House, the Greek revival home of the "Father of the Texas Navy," Samuel May Williams, who also was Texas's first banker. The house, fabricated in Maine and shipped by schooner to Galveston, has been restored by the Galveston Historical Society to illustrate the homey atmosphere created by a recliner chair and piano, delicate china, beautiful rugs, brick fireplaces, and other fine furnishings. The Bishop's

Palace, constructed in 1886 of native Texas granite, white limestone, and red sandstone to a design by Nicholas Clayton, is the only Texas structure on the American Institute of Architects' list of the nation's 100 most outstanding buildings. It gets its current name from the time it served as the home of the Roman Catholic Bishop of the Galveston–Houston Diocese.

St. Joseph's Church, a frame structure with an ornate gothic interior, was raised in 1859. It is leased by the Galveston Historical Society as a museum depicting the city's religious history. The restored 1894 Opera House is used for a Jazz Festival in November and other events.

Galveston was among the ports visited by the square-rigged, iron-hulled sailing bark *Elissa* when she roamed the seas for almost a century in search of cargoes, first as a legitimate merchantman and then as a smuggler. Launched in 1877 in Scotland, the 411-ton ship was condemned in 1974, saved from destruction for scrap, and restored to emphasize the city's long role as a seaport. It is generally tied up at Pier 21 near the Strand and can be visited. On occasion, however, the three-masted vessel represents Texas at such festivities as the Statue of Liberty Centennial of Sail on July 4, 1986. The ambience of 19th-century cruising is revived also by *The Colonel*, a replica of a sidewheeler whose crew wears naval uniforms like those worn in the 1830s.

Galveston's colorful history is explored at the Galveston County Historical Museum, located in a 1919 neoclassical building which once held a bank. Displays range from Karankara Indian artifacts and information on the Texas navy to a 1905 general store and a mock-up of a train station.

Ashton Villa was built in the Italiante style in 1859. Its owner was a wealthy businessman and civic leader, James Moreau Brown.

The parlor of Ashton Villa.

Along Oklahoma Avenue, one can find many of the restored Victorian commercial buildings that form the heart of Guthrie's historic district.

(Opposite) This cupola identifies the Gray Brothers building on Oklahoma Avenue. Built in 1890, it served as the Bank of Indian Territory until 1907. Today, it houses a craft store and a book shop.

Oklahoma acknowledges its past role as the Indian Territory in a number of ways. The name of the state derives from Indian words meaning "red people." The state seal incorporates a number of native American symbols. And the state flag includes an Osage warrior's shield.

Such harmony between the races was a long time in coming. Although Oklahoma had been settled by Indians long before the Spanish explorer Francisco Vásquez de Coronado passed through in 1541, it was only sparsely inhabited by the Osage, Kiowa, Comanche, and Apache tribes when it was acquired by the United States in 1803 as part of the Louisiana Purchase. When the mass westward migration from the Eastern states began in the 1830s and 1840s, the preferred routes bypassed it. Consequently, it was conveniently designated "Indian Territory" in the first half of the 19th century and chosen as the home of relocated Eastern and Gulf Coast tribes. In other words, many of the native Americans living in the lush rolling hills of Oklahoma in the late 19th century had been forced to resettle there. Most of the land within the present state boundaries was divided into 19 segments of various sizes, each given to a tribe or tribal grouping. The panhandle was originally the largest strip of unallocated land.

The separate tribal enclaves did not remain inviolate for

Wagons and horses jammed this Guthrie intersection in 1896. A view of the same locale today seems calm by comparison.

long. The cattle trails along which steers were driven from Texas to the railroad centers of Kansas and Missouri for shipment east crisscrossed the Indian Territory. Among them were the two branches of the Shawnee Trail, the first of the great cattle routes; the Chisholm Trail, the most famous, named for Cherokee Indian trader Jesse Chisholm; and the Great Western Trail, which ended at Dodge City, Kansas. Rustlers and swindlers followed the trail herds. The Marlow brothers, for example, were notorious for stealing cattle, returning them to their owners, and collecting a reward for finding them.

While the periodic incursions of the herds aggravated the Indians, it was the decision in 1889 to open up a segment of Indian Territory to white settlement that forever changed the face of Oklahoma. Five "land rushes" were made prior to 1895. The first involved unallocated land; subsequent rushes opened parcels previously given to the Sac, Fox, Pottawatomie–Shawnee, Cheyenne, Arapaho, Cherokee, and Kickapoo tribes. These land-settlement schemes created the unique Caucasian–Indian population mix that characterizes today's Oklahoma.

Guthrie, near the center of the state at a point where the railroad crossed the Cimarron River, was a land registration station for thousands of those who staked out sites in the first land rush. It was an event that captured the imagination of the world—so much so that even the European press covered it. Gunfire at noon on April 22, 1889, initiated the frantic race across the green plains that has been imprinted into the minds of many Americans by Hollywood. There were riders on horseback. There were families in covered wagons carrying all their possessions as they hastened to stake claims on choice sites. And there were businessmen in wagons full of lumber for hastily constructed stores where the supplies carried on yet other wagons could be sold. By sundown on land-rush day, all the lots in Guthrie and

The Saloon

Arguably no place of business is more closely associated with the Old West than the saloon, that ubiquitous den of pleasure populated by dance-hall girls, honky-tonk pianos, gamblers, and cowboys. One such establishment was the Blue Belle in Guthrie, Oklahoma. Here in a rather substantial brick structure erected in 1899, Oklahoma ranchers, such as Zack Mulhall, mingled freely with notorious outlaws like Emmett Dalton and Henry Starr. But the most famous figure to be associated with the establishment is Tom Mix, that stalwart hero of the silent cowboy movies who, with his wonder horse Tony, enchanted filmgoers everywhere. He arrived in Guthrie in 1902 as a deserter from the U.S. Army, became the Blue Belle's bartender and number-one orderly, and later signed on as a cowhand at the 101 Ranch, where he was discovered by a film crew. When they aren't remembering the "King of the Cowboys," local historians like to speculate on what was once upstairs of the Blue Belle. Popular theory maintains that it contained a bordello, or if not, at least a walkway that extended from the building's upper environs to the Elks' Hotel across the alley. There Guthrie's men of stature could mingle with ladies of the evening without using the front door (and thus avoid the risk of being seen). Statehood came in 1907 and with it the ban on drinking that brought the Blue Belle's raucous days to an end. Prohibition was repealed in 1959, however, and the bar reopened as Edna's Lounge. In 1977, it was again christened the Blue Belle in honor of its notorious past. Today, the saloon looks much as it did in those wild days before statehood, with the original tile work, woodwork, metal ceiling, and bar reminding visitors of the days when good old Tom served all comers.

THE EXTERIOR (left) AND INTERIOR (above) OF GUTHRIE'S BLUE BELLE

other cities were taken. Thanks to its key location, the registration center soon boasted a temporary tent-and-board city of approximately 20,000 settlers.

A provisional territorial government was quickly established, but it did not receive legal status until 1890, at which time Guthrie was chosen as its capital. Guthrie was also a market town for big ranches, such as the 80,000-acre tract owned by Zack Mulhall, while the vast land that surrounded the town provided a favorite haunt for outlaws. Bank and train robberies were commonplace. Among the most notorious gang in the area was that of Bill Doolin, which rode without restraint until Doolin himself was ambushed by a posse that included U.S. Deputy Marshal Heck Thomas. From this era also emerged some of the West's most famous female bandits, Rose of Cimarron (Rose E. Dunn), Belle Starr, and Cattle Annie among them.

Many of the colorful figures of the area later either lent their names to or starred in the Wild West shows which began touring about 1900. Rancher Zack Mulhall was among those sponsoring shows; he starred his daughter, Lucille, as the first "cowgirl." She was a favorite of President Theodore Roosevelt during the 15 years that the show traveled.

Guthrie continued to prosper as a result of all this activity and became, for a time, one of the most influential cities in Oklahoma. By 1906, when the lines of nine railroads ran through the city, it had about 12,000 inhabitants. However, the future state remained divided into Indian and white territories, each entertaining ideas of statehood. Congress, however, would admit only a unified Oklahoma, so the Indian leaders finally acquiesced to joint statehood. Oklahoma became the 46th state

Advertisements for a modern-day shopping center use graphic elements that recall the bygone age when Guthrie was Oklahoma's bustling state capital.

on November 16, 1907, with Guthrie as its first capital. In 1910, the capital was moved to Oklahoma City, largely as a result of partisan political intrigue.

Today, the original townsite in downtown Guthrie is a National Historic Landmark. Its 1,483 acres are said to comprise the largest district on the National Register of Historic Places. The section has largely been restored to its appearance of 1910, Guthrie's last year as the state capital.

The lifestyle of some of Guthrie's prominent citizens during the late-territorial and early-statehood periods can be viewed at four residences on a historic homes tour organized by the Guthrie Chamber of Commerce and the Logan County Historical Society. While these sites are presently occupied, their owners admit visitors during the holiday season. The oldest stop on the tour is a house built in 1891 and occupied from 1897 to 1909 by Territorial Governor Cassius M. Barnes. A tape recording of reminiscences by a grandson of Governor Barnes enlivens viewings of the interior rooms, which have been restored to their appearance when the governor lived there.

Museums in Guthrie include the State Capital Publishing Museum, a restored 1902 commercial building with intricate grillwork and woodwork where Oklahoma's first newspaper was published; and the Oklahoma Territorial Museum, filled with artifacts and historical displays depicting the territory's colorful path to statehood.

A turn-of-the-century ambiance prevails at the Harrison House. It was constructed in 1903 as the Eager-Hirzel Bank, but now serves as a bed and breakfast.

The notorious female bandit Belle Starr, shown here in 1887 at Fort Smith, Arkansas. She was murdered two years later by an unknown assailant.

SANTA FE
NEW MEXICO

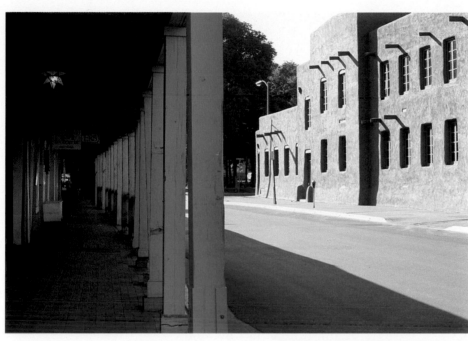

Narrow streets in Santa Fe's historic district, like Palace Avenue shown here, lead to the Plaza, the focal point of the city's history and culture since Santa Fe was founded in 1610.

(*Opposite*) The architecture of this Presbyterian Church is typical of the traditional Spanish-adobe style that dominates the old section of Santa Fe.

They struggled down the narrow, dusty road, their whips cracking like gunshots over the heads of mules and oxen. They moved slowly, doggedly, not smartly. But these trail-weary *Americanos* were a welcome sight to the people of Santa Fe, who recently had won their independence from Spain.

The goods in the wagons had cost $150 in Franklin, Missouri, where the small band of drovers led by William Becknell had begun their 900-mile journey on September 1, 1821. Luck had brought them there; the small party had driven west to trade with Indians, but it had been encouraged by Mexican dragoons to try Santa Fe. They received $700 for their loads, a handsome profit in those days for 10 weeks' work, and Becknell quickly organized another caravan which arrived in 1822. This one sold its goods for a 2,000 percent profit.

The route Becknell laid out became the Santa Fe Trail, one of the legendary thoroughfares in American history. As the years passed, larger and larger caravans, carrying settlers as well as cargo, risked attack by Indians and bandits, rainstorms, drought, and other hazards of the wilderness to follow the trail westward. Within a generation of Becknell's arrival, a single train parking at Santa Fe's Plaza might have consisted of hundreds of wagons and might have carried goods worth as much as half a million dollars.

(*Opposite*) Indians from the pueblos near Santa Fe display their handicrafts on the long portico of the Palace of the Governors.

Santa Fe's role as the hub of what is now the southwestern United States had been established long before Becknell's daring drive. Founded in 1610, Santa Fe is the oldest capital in North America and the oldest American community west of the Mississippi. It did not achieve such longevity easily; the city has been buffeted by uprisings, revolts, cruelty, and invasion during five definable epochs: pre-Spanish conquest, circa 1050–1610; early Spanish settlement and Indian revolt, 1610–1692; established Spanish empire, 1692–1821; Mexican period, 1821–1848; and American period, 1846 to the present.

The ancient Pueblo Indians, whose descendants still live in more than 20 pueblos in northeast New Mexico, were the first to build on the site of Santa Fe. Between 1050 and 1150, they raised several villages, including Kaupoge, or "place of shell beads near water," but abandoned them about 200 years before the Spanish conquistador Francisco Vásquez de Coronado explored the region in 1540. Little evidence of these villages remains.

Santa Fe (the full name was La Villa Real de Santa Fe de San Francisco de Assisi, or the Royal Town of the Holy Faith of Saint Francis of Assisi) was founded in 1610 by the conquistador Pedro de Peralta. The city quickly became the political and social hub of all Spanish territory in the Southwest, but the orderly, comfortable lifestyle which the city enjoyed was interrupted on numerous occasions. In 1680, the Pueblo Indians revolted against the harsh Spanish rule and the Spaniards' efforts to convert them; in one of the few successful Indian uprisings, they killed about 400 colonists and drove 2,000 more back to Mexico. The city was retaken by Diego de Vargas in 1692.

The successful Mexican revolt against Spanish rule in 1821 opened the way for settlement by American citizens. It also resulted in a more open trade policy toward the United States. The United States occupied Santa Fe in 1846, during the Mexican War, and gained permanent possession of New Mexico and California under the Treaty of Guadalupe Hidalgo, which ended the war in 1848.

Many aspects of the city's varied history are still visible in and around Santa Fe Plaza, focal point of city life since the beginning. Laid out as a parade ground for military activities and religious processions, it has been used to celebrate virtually every major event in the city's history, regardless of which flag (Spanish, Mexican, United States, Confederate) might be flying at

For more than 250 years, governors administered the affairs of New Mexico from this simple office. The Palace of the Governors is the oldest public building in continuous use in the United States.

The Mission System

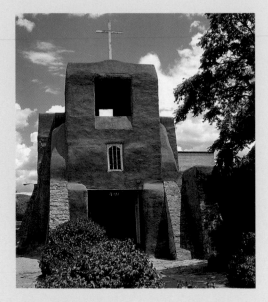

For Spain, the chance to convert the Indians to Roman Catholicism was one of the prime attractions of the New World, second only to the lure of gold. "We rejoiced to find so many pagans upon whom the light of our holy faith was about to dawn," wrote one enthusiastic priest in 1782. To achieve its objective, the crown established a large network of missions throughout the Southwest and California, each typically staffed by two Franciscan monks. At first, the Indians were attracted to the missions out of curiosity and by the lure of food, clothing, and shelter. But, once they were baptized, they were forbidden to practice their ancient ways. They were also forced to live at the mission, to till its lands, and

to learn skills, like carpentry and candle-making. "The confusion in the heads and hearts of these poor people who can only know how to mimic some external ceremonies must indeed be very great," wrote one non-Spanish observer in 1816. All told, probably no more than 10 percent of the indigenous Indians were converted. But the system had a devastating impact upon their numbers, for they were exposed for the first time to diseases like measles and small pox for which they had no immunity. Two-thirds of California's Indian population had succumbed to such diseases by the mid-1830s. Shortly thereafter, the system came to an end. Mexico, which had won its independence from Spain and inherited the mother country's colonies in North America, sold the mission lands, thereby eliminating the means by which the missionaries had supported their charges. But the sanctuaries remained, no longer as outposts for converts, but rather as parish churches.

THE INTERIOR (left) AND THE EXTERIOR (above) OF SANTA FE'S CHAPEL OF SAN MIGUEL

the time. It was also the terminus of the Santa Fe Trail, used as a market, and as the setting for public executions and floggings.

Although the Plaza is no longer the geographic center of the city, almost every visitor to Santa Fe stops to enjoy the square's old-world charm, enhanced by cottonwood trees. One of the major structures facing the Plaza is the Palace of the Governors, the oldest public building in continuous use in the United States. This *palacio* has witnessed all the drama and sacrifice that spice Santa Fe's history; conquerors came and went here and governments rose and fell while clerks and bureaucrats struggled with the minutiae of government. Today its rooms house displays of historical relics from the Museum of New Mexico. Outside, Indians from pueblos near Santa Fe display their handicrafts on the long portico.

Around the Plaza, the downtown section and abutting residential areas are dominated by Spanish-Pueblo Revival architecture. Even new buildings in the historic area, many of which house trendy shops and hotels, are required by law to use traditional Indian and Spanish colonial architectural motifs.

Santa Fe's beautiful Roman Catholic churches date from various periods in the city's history. Among those near the Plaza are the 1869 French Romanesque-style Cathedral of St. Francis of Assisi, which incorporates a section of an earlier church burned in the Pueblo revolt; and the Chapel of Our Lady of Guadalupe, built in 1795. Constructed in 1878, Our Lady of Light Chapel, also known as the Loretto Chapel, has a spiral staircase that leads to the choir loft and is joined without nails or screws. San Miguel Chapel, the first church in the city, is one of the focal points of the Barrio de Analco, as the old section south of the Rio de Santa Fe is known. The thick adobe walls of the mission survived Indian torches during the uprising of 1680. The church was rebuilt in 1710.

The Cathedral of St. Francis of
Assisi as it looks today and as it
looked in the early 1890s, when
it was still under construction.
The cornerstone was laid in
1869.

Sena Plaza, not far from the main square, has an ambience similar to that of the more-famous quarter. The hacienda there has been adapted to house galleries, shops, and restaurants, and the former courtyard is a park.

The ruins of an American adobe fort, whose walls were 5 feet thick and 9 feet high, stand atop a hill about 600 yards northeast of the Plaza. Fort Marcy, built in 1846 during the Mexican-American War occupation period, was the first American fort in the Southwest.

Through periods of violence and peace, Santa Feans have maintained a civilized perspective that has elevated cultural activities to a necessity. Premier among the city's cultural offerings is the world-renowned Santa Fe Opera with its glittering performance season. There is also the Santa Fe Symphony and presentations of the historical drama *Santa Fe Spirit*. And the city

Conquistador Don Francisco Vásques de Coronado, shown in this 1920 mural by Gerald Cassidy, claimed New Mexico for Spain 70 years before Santa Fe was founded.

has an astonishing 150 art galleries. The Fiesta of Santa Fe, with its historical pageantry, dance, arts and crafts, and fireworks, has been held every September for the past 275 years. Other major annual events include the Indian Market in late August and the Spanish Market in July.

The Public Library was built in 1908. It is presently under renovation, but is scheduled to re-open in 1991 as the town's history library and photo archive.

The Montaño store was built in the 1860s by Jose and Josefa Montaño. It featured a saloon as well as general merchandise.

(*Opposite*) The Torreón, a round stone fort constructed in about 1885, was strategically located in Lincoln to provide security for the town's inhabitants during Indian raids.

Y ou had to be there to understand it. The Lincoln County War—which made the town of Lincoln one of the legendary towns of the Old West—was an armed test of strength between two rival merchant groups for economic control of southeastern New Mexico. It began with the murder of a naive English rancher named John Tunstall and ended with the murder of his business partner Alexander McSween. The more than five months between those incidents was a confusing period of merciless killing and destruction during which all of the following, and more, occurred:

- The merchants fought each other with small armies of hired hands, some of them former friends now on opposite sides.

- The legal system was subordinated to personal interests by those wielding power, but at different times some men on each side were deputized to bring in men on the other side. A sheriff was ambushed on the streets of the town of Lincoln.

- One of the principal antagonists was flushed from his house in Lincoln by fire and shot down as he came out.

- The commander of nearby Fort Stanton was induced to use his troops to support one side, but survived an inquiry.

- One territorial governor was sacked for not resolving the crisis, and his successor, author and general Lew Wallace, promised Billy the Kid immunity but did nothing when the Kid was convicted in Mesilla of murder and sentenced to hang in Lincoln.

(Opposite) The interior of the Montaño store. Today it houses a Spanish-heritage museum with a bar, a small store, and the proprietor's living quarters.

William Bonney, also known as "Billy the Kid," earned his reputation as a gunfighter during the merciless bloodbath known as the Lincoln County War.

A former bartender, Pat Garrett was elected Lincoln County sheriff in 1880. Although he and Billy the Kid were friends, he killed the outlaw in July 1881 after Billy escaped from his jail.

Lincoln County began as a quiet Hispanic farming and sheepherding region, where the main concern of the isolated *placitas* along the Rio Bonito was raids by the Apache Indians. The "war" stemmed primarily from the conflict between two local entrepreneurs, cattle baron John Chisum and merchant L. G. Murphy. In addition, the size and isolation of the county, which after 1878 was larger than South Carolina, made it ideal for outlaws, who could lose themselves in the thousands of square miles of rugged river valleys, high pastures, and forested foothills in the shadow of the 12,000-foot Sierra Blanca mountains. Before the "war," the outlaws, in comic opera fashion, regularly rustled cattle from the largest cattlemen, then sold animals taken from the first to the second, and vice versa.

In the end, the "war" proved costly to everyone concerned. The antagonists' financial losses were staggering. The county was burdened with the expense of numerous deputies, many of them gunfighters, some of whom remained after their badges were lifted to prey on people and herds. The economy of the town of Lincoln, the county seat and principal population center, was wrecked. In addition, the town sustained physical damage during a five-day shootout that more or less settled the affair.

The romance that surrounded Billy the Kid has proved to be the most enduring aspect of the "war." Billy's early life hardly bore the markings of a future Western legend. Born in New

Frontier Medicine

A doctor in the Old West had to cover a very broad territory, ministering not only to the needs of the townfolk but also to those of the farmers and ranchers in the surrounding area. Patients that didn't have cash or mineral ore paid in commodities - produce, fowl, and livestock being the most frequent cash substitutes. He had to be a general practioner par excellence, capable of diagnosing illness, and performing surgery - including amputations - without modern anesthetic. Moreover, conditions were not usually conducive to the practice of good medicine. The streets of most burgeoning Western towns were peppered with horse droppings and flies. The streams that provided drinking water were often polluted. And insects, coming into homes through open windows, spread malaria or ague through many a Western community. Epidemics, such as small pox, diphtheria, and cholera, were common too. There were no hospitals; doctors maintained offices in their homes. They also maintained pharmacies, where they mixed remedies by combining bottled ingredients with herbs that they grew themselves. The staples of any physician's medicine chest were the concoctions, such as Dr. John Bull's Vegetable Worm Destroyer, Dr. J. Bradfield's Female Regulator, and Hosteller's Celebrated Stomach Bitters, that were little more than hard liquor. But doctors, faced with few alternatives, did the best they could. Of course "best" is a relative term. Many doctors trekked West because they had been unable to make a living back home. There were those, however, who just fell in love with a place and stayed. A case in point is Dr. Thomas L. McCarty, who stopped in Dodge City, Kansas, while en route to Denver in 1872. He was so taken with the bustling cowtown that he set up a practice in a local drug store, and spent his life there, giving birth to a son who also became a doctor and founding the town hospital.

THE INTERIOR OF DR. WOOD'S HOUSE, LINCOLN

York City and christened Henry McCarty, Billy had come to New Mexico with his mother following his father's death. He adapted easily to the wild ways of the West; by his teens, he had drifted into a life of crime after killing an Arizona man in an argument. He took the name William Bonney and ran around with toughs like Charlie Bowdre and Tom O'Folliard, who accepted him as the leader of their minor rustling activities. His nickname, "Billy the Kid," was often shortened to simply "the Kid" by those who knew him best.

Billy became involved in the Lincoln County War when his employer, John Tunstall, was shot down in cold blood on the road into Lincoln by a sheriff's posse. When Sheriff William Brady did nothing about the shooting, Tunstall partisans were deputized by Justice of the Peace John B. Wilson. Sheriff Brady was shot from ambush by Billy the Kid and other Tunstall partisans, and the bitter war of revenge and counter retaliation fueled by personal animosities was on. The gun battle in Lincoln ended with the decimation of the pro-Tunstall forces, the exhaustion of the Murphy forces on the other side, and a general amnesty. Lincoln had already returned to its usual raucous condition by the time Sheriff Garrett shot Billy the Kid in Fort Sumner on July 14, 1881.

The town of Lincoln declined after the county seat was moved to Carri-

The first building in Lincoln opened as a schoolhouse in October 1885 and remained in use well into the 20th century. It is now the Community Church.

At the outset of the Lincoln County War, this adobe courthouse housed the Murphy-Dolan Store on the first floor and a jail on the second.

133

The highway through Lincoln passes about 40 historic structures and sites, just as the original dirt road did in the earlier photograph, taken in around 1886.

zoza, on the railroad line. Indeed, it had only 60 inhabitants before a modern revival began in 1976 with the assistance of the Lincoln County Heritage Trust, which works with residents and the State Monuments Division to re-create an Old West atmosphere.

The town of Lincoln still would be recognizable to Billy the Kid or Jimmy Dolan, the honcho of the Murphy faction. The highway follows the original curving route through the town, passing about 40 historic buildings and sites, most of them adobe structures, about two-thirds of which are owned by the trust and the New Mexico State Monuments Division. The town is classified as a National Historic Landmark, with a commission that controls constructions and alterations within an area around Lincoln that is a mile wide and 10 miles long.

Among the historic structures open to visitors are the adobe courthouse-jail, which at the start of the "war" housed the Murphy–Dolan Store on the first floor and the jail on the second (currently it is a history museum); the 1877 Tunstall Store, which re-creates the firm of the period; Dr. Wood's House, furnished as both a residence and an office/surgery, as it was during the physician's lifetime; and the San Juan Mission, built about 1887. Other major buildings include the reconstructed Lincoln Hotel (now the Worley Hotel); The Torreon, a round stone fort constructed about 1855 to provide security from Indian raids; and the Gallegos House, dating from 1901, houses some offices of the Lincoln County Heritage Trust.

The adobe-style Historical Center, built in 1981, houses exhibits on the Lincoln County War and relics from the area's varied inhabitants, including the Apaches, the Buffalo (black) soldiers, the Spanish, and the cowboys. An outdoor drama, *The Last Escape of Billy the Kid,* is reenacted every year by regional actors during the Old Lincoln Days in early August.

A monument on U.S. Route 70 near Glencoe marks the site where Tunstall was killed.

The San Juan-Bautista Mission, built in about 1887. The sanctuary, seen above, is typical of the modest yet attractive style found in most frontier churches.

One of the "Clanton's" pauses for a moment before heading over to the O. K. Corral.

(*Opposite*) The Bird Cage Theatre, which opened in Tombstone in 1881, was once described as the "wildest, wickedest night spot between Basin Street and the Barbary Coast."

Ed Schieffelin was in most ways a typical prospector: he was incorrigible and he was optimistic. He had prospected all over the West, taking steady jobs only to raise new grubstakes in his search for precious metals. And each time he set out on a new dig, he was certain that it would be the Mother Lode. So it was when he ventured into the wilds of southeastern Arizona. Those who knew the region thought differently; they said he would find only his tombstone.

When he struck it big—ore samples from his Toughnut Mine assayed at $2,000 a ton and the ore actually was much richer—even dedicated cattle ranchers gained a new appreciation for the area's mineral potential. A few years later, a dozen major mines were producing a steady stream of ore bearing gold and silver in various quantities.

Schieffelin differed from most prospectors in one regard. He did not follow the familiar cycle of discovering silver, selling the claim to someone else, spending the money, and then returning to prospecting. Schieffelin found so much silver that he could organize his own company and fulfill the dream of every prospector—to become filthy rich. He was an active and respected leader in the community which sprang up to serve the new strike—Tombstone.

Named for the taunts aimed at Schieffelin—that he would

(*Opposite*) Disputes that didn't end in gunfire were adjudicated in this courtroom which was constructed in 1882. The courthouse now houses Wyatt Earp memorabilia.

find only his grave—Tombstone was initially prized for its grazing land, but it remained largely unsettled due to the threat of marauding Apaches. In Schieffelin's wake, however, came a horde of prospectors. The scent of a big strike made them oblivious to the dangers the area offered. Indeed, they fanned out like ants across the rolling foothills and into the nearby mountains, but most of the rich strikes were located near Tombstone. Some of the most famous mines in the West, Toughnut, Lucky Cuss, Contention, Emerald, and Good Enough among them, derive from this place and era. Mine shafts even extended under the town.

Tombstone's historic area reflects the community in the 1880s, when it epitomized the West at its wickedest. The 1882 brick jail, whose first floor was occupied by a fire company, and the Wells Fargo Museum and General Store each in its own way recalls the era when desperadoes made the shipment of silver and gold to Tucson uncertain. Boot Hill Cemetery's fame does not rest solely on the graves of the losers in the O.K. Corral shootout, the Clantons and McLaurys; alongside numerous gunmen and desperadoes is the poor fellow whose headstone reads "Hanged by Mistake."

The 1881 Bird Cage Theatre, which featured prostitutes in cages suspended from the ceiling, operated for nine years without closing its doors. It was once described as the "wildest, wickedest night spot between Basin Street and the Barbary Coast," a true example of the Tombstone lifestyle during the mining town's heyday. Now a Historic Landmark of the American West, the Bird Cage was sealed after flooding in the mines virtually shut down the town. As a result, many of its original furnishings have been preserved, including

"DOC" HOLLIDAY

The Gunfighters

Wyatt Earp . . . "Wild Bill" Hickok . . . Billy the Kid . . . Jesse James . . . these men were gunfighters, the elite in a society where firearms were freely used to settle disputes. A gunfighter was simply one who could shoot. He might be an outlaw, a cowboy, a gambler, or even a keeper of the peace. How many men did the celebrated pistoleers kill? No one knows for sure but in many cases their deeds were exaggerated. It was said, for example, that Bat Masterson shot a dozen men when he was sheriff of Ford County, Kansas, but there is no evidence that he actually killed anyone. As for Wyatt Earp, his reputation as a gunman stems largely from a single incident, the gunfight at the O.K. Corral. But few shootists - as Texan Clay Allison called himself - discouraged

notoriety. Having a reputation was a valuable asset. Moreover, the notorious formed a unique fraternity. They rarely fought with one another; there was always someone less risky to attack. Their favorite handgun was the Colt 45 revolver. With it a "sure shot" could hit a man in a gunfight at 15 yards. To do so, however, required long hours of practice. "When he could draw, cock, and fire all in one smooth, lighting-quick movement," wrote Bat Masterson, "he could then detach his mind from that movement, and concentrate on accuracy." Wyatt Earp maintained that the best way to win a shoot-out was to take one's time. He must have known what he was talking about. He lived to be 81 years old and died of natural causes.

THE "GUNFIGHT" AT THE OK CORRAL

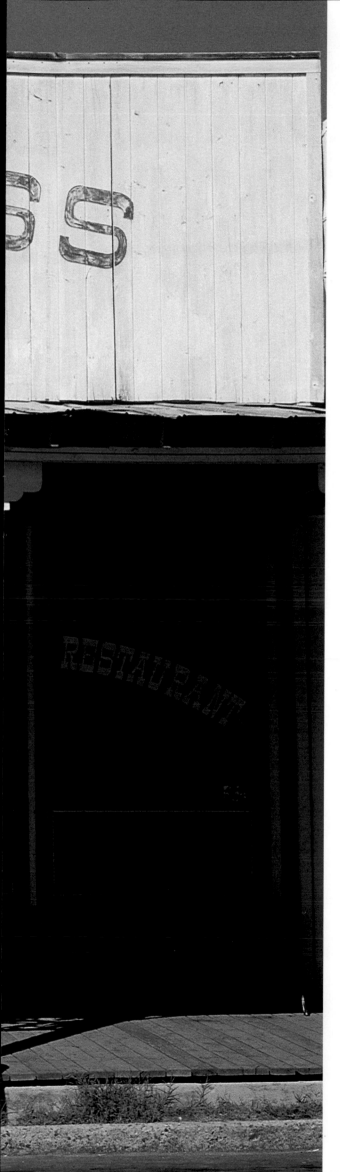

the handsome cherry wood bar, the painting of Fatima (punctured by six bullet holes), the stage, chandeliers, and curtains. The card table and chairs in the dirt-floor basement recall a poker game that ran without pause for eight years and five months. The Crystal Palace, the most famous of the town's saloons when Tombstone was in full swing, is restored to its 1879 appearance, including the long bar, which in the 1880s stayed open all night.

The good earth which produced such frenzy is still mined, but now it's just for show. For example, the Good Enough Mine, an 1881 Schieffelin discovery whose shafts run under the town, enables visitors to see how silver was extracted in the Old West.

Hell-raising Tombstone, like many mining towns, had a gentler, law-abiding side. The "good" people of the community were entertained at Schieffelin Hall, a large adobe structure which has been restored to its original appearance.

The Lucky Cuss Saloon is named for one of the famous mines near Tombstone which produced untold millions in gold and silver.

Many of the fixtures and decorative elements in the Bird Cage Theatre are original. They have survived for over a century without damage because the theater was sealed for many years after the mines flooded.

The Rose Tree Inn, which opened in 1882 is named for a *lady banksia* rosebush planted behind the inn more than a century ago by the wife of a mine manager. Today the inn is a museum open to the public and the rose bush is the largest in the world, according to *Ripley's Believe It or Not*.

The famous Wyatt Earp earned much of his reputation while serving as a deputy marshal in Tombstone. His brother Virgil was marshal.

They worshipped at St. Paul's Episcopal Church, built in 1882, the oldest Protestant church still standing in Arizona. And they settled their disputes at the 1882 brick Courthouse, now a state park housing historical items, including Wyatt Earp memorabilia.

Tombstone was rowdy from the day it opened. Two-thirds of the buildings held saloons or gambling halls, many of which remained open around-the-clock to satisfy the desires of the prospectors, miners, cowboys, and those who hoped to benefit from their labors. The night air on Allen Street was filled with the sounds of raucous men at play. Occasionally, tempers flared and guns blazed. Soon, a larger cemetery was needed.

Some of the most legendary characters in the West lent their names to Tombstone's colorful history. The most famous, of course, were the Earp brothers and "Doc" Holliday, who defeated the Clantons and McLaurys in the classic gunfight at the O.K. Corral (today re-created by lifesize mannequins). Deputy Marshal Wyatt Earp and his brothers Virgil and Morgan already had substantial reputations in the West by the time they arrived in Tombstone, but the 60-second shootout brought them national attention. Historians disagree about the motives behind the fight; sentiment in the community was divided between the Earp and Clanton factions (many in Tombstone wanted to lynch the Earps after the fight), but the Earps and their sidekick "Doc" Holliday were exonerated after a judicial hearing. After leaving Arizona in 1883, Wyatt served as a lawman elsewhere, including Alaska, but miraculously lived through it all and died in Los Angeles in 1929 at age 80.

Tombstone's earliest settlers sought to achieve an orderly expansion of the town by creating a development plan, but progress proved to be as unpredict

able as the size of a silver deposit. Although Frémont Street was supposed to be the main drag, Allen Street actually became the heart of the town. Such aberrations did not impede growth in the least. But, by 1883, with underground water seepage hampering mine operations and pumping costs becoming prohibitive, the town once described as "too tough to die" almost disappeared. Tombstone hung on as a virtual ghost town until after World War II, when it was brought back to life by a daring group of 20th-century merchants and residents eager to preserve their heritage. The resultant tourism has given Tombstone almost as much prosperity as did the mines during the boom-town days.

This firehouse was established in 1880 as the station for Tombstone Engine Co. No. 1, a volunteer brigade.

The Far West

The Spring City Tabernacle, completed in 1914, is in the Romanesque revival style.

(*Opposite*) The design of this school, built in 1899, is often described as Victorian eclectic. It houses a small museum, operated by the Daughters of Utah Pioneers, which is open to the public during the town's annual Heritage Day celebration.

(*Preceding pages*) Virginia City, Nevada.

One night in the 1890s, Butch Cassidy rode down the dusty Main Street of Spring City, Utah, and turned onto 4th Street. He rode straight to the door of Circuit Judge Jacob Johnson. The judge walked onto the balcony above his front porch and greeted the outlaw. They chatted for a few minutes, and the judge told Cassidy to have a cold one from the pantry to clear the dust from his throat.

Cassidy, an incorrigible but careful outlaw who planned bank robberies skillfully and always inspected his route of escape, did not interrupt the placid life of Spring City the way he did so many other towns, including Telluride, Colorado. Born Robert LeRoy Parker, Cassidy may have had an agreement with Judge Johnson; the outlaw was widely known to be a man of his word. Besides, there was little loot in tiny Spring City, a pastoral community tucked away in the Wasatch Plateau about 60 miles southeast of Provo. So he just left Spring City as he found it, riding away toward his lair, Robber's Roost, near the outlaw trail that ran through eastern Utah. The wild and isolated sections of the Beehive State were among the last haunts of the outlaws.

This incident is local legend, but like most legends it probably has some basis in fact. At the least, it is not inconsistent with well-documented history. Cassidy, the leader

of the Wild Bunch, one of the last of the outlaw gangs of the Old West, roamed the rugged hills and river valleys of eastern and central Utah for many years before he and the Sundance Kid migrated to South America.

Other legends are less plausible, and indeed exist in several variations, but they still have some currency in the region around Spring City. Some people question whether Cassidy and the Sundance Kid died in a hail of gunfire in South America, as many historians claim. Cassidy, their story goes, lived out his life in the Northwest, whereas the Sundance Kid stayed in Spring City awhile and then was hustled off to prison for shooting the marshal of nearby Mount Pleasant.

Spring City was no stranger to violence before the Wild Bunch arrived. Indeed, it was sacked by Indians in 1853 during the Wakara War, little more than a year after the Mormon apostle James Allred and 14 families from the Salt Lake City area established a new colony known as Canal Creek. Under Indian pressure, the settlers retreated to Manti and soon helped establish Fort Ephraim. But Mormons were settlers, interested in permanent use of the land—in contrast to most of the argonauts who overran the Old West—and they were soon back at Canal Creek, now called Spring City, to take advantage of abundant springs that helped make the land productive. Their placid lifestyle was interrupted again in the 1860s, but only briefly, by the Blackhawk War.

The community's name was changed in the 1860s to Spring Town in recognition of the life-giving springs. It became Spring City in 1870 when it was incorporated, and remained prosperous until the middle of the 20th century, when relocation of U.S. Route 89 left the community isolated. Loss of the highway was a mixed blessing; it helped preserve the old buildings but reduced

An interior view of the Jacob Johnson house. This residence also served as the judge's office.

In 1895, John R. Baxter and Robert Blair opened this store, which stocked grocery items, coal oil, sewing materials, and articles of clothing. In 1924, it was sold to Baxter's son-in-law, Clarence Schofield, who renamed it Schofield Mercantile.

the population to about 400. The mid-1970s saw an influx of young families and those seeking summer homes, which about doubled the number of residents.

An opportunity for the tourist to be ahead of the crowd is rare these days, but one exists at Spring City. It is perhaps the least known of the legendary towns of the Old West. However, Spring City bows to no place in its historical value. It has been on the National Register of Historic Places since 1981, primarily because it illustrates the "techniques of Mormon town planning in Utah" whereby blocks were laid

off so that each house and ancillary structures formed a more or less self-contained unit. The large number of buildings, barns, sheds, and other ancillaries from the last half of the 19th century, and particularly the closing decades, preserves the "feel" of a Mormon community of the period.

The oldest structure is the circa 1865 Orson Hyde House on South Main Street. Hyde, an apostle sent to Sanpete County in 1858 by Mormon leader Brigham Young, lived in the stone vernacular house with one of his six wives.

The house visited by Butch Cassidy, which 7th District Judge Johnson used as an office and courtroom as well as a

home, is among the most interesting architecturally. The main part of the house was constructed in the Greek revival style in 1875, while the rear, in the Victorian style, was added in 1892. According to some townspeople, the judge's ghost now and then rattles a coffee cup in the kitchen and leaves the odor of cigars in the parlor. The Queen Anne–style stone house across the street looks more like marble than stone, thanks to the workmanship of Jens Peter Carlson, a skilled mason

Judge Jacob Johnson met Butch
Cassidy in this house. The main
section of the structure was constructed in the Greek revival style
in 1875; the rear, in the Victorian
style, was added in 1892.

The Wild Bunch, led by Butch
Cassidy (*seated right*), was among
the last of the West's legendary
outlaw gangs. One of their hide-
outs, known as Robbers Roost,
was in eastern Utah.

who also worked on the Salt Lake City Temple and the Spring City Tabernacle. After inspecting the addition to Judge Johnson's house, Carlson decided he could do better and, in 1896, began shaping and smoothing stones so carefully that the space between them measures about ⅛ inch.

Other 19th-century buildings include: the federal-style, two-story James Allred House, built in 1874 of redwood siding hauled from California; the granary, circa 1875, where the Mormon women's society stored food for the needy; and the Old City Hall, mainly Greek revival in style, which was completed in 1893. The 1870s Peter Jensen House, relocated from Sevier County by the Utah Historical Society to prevent its destruction, is typical of the log structures raised by Swedish newcomers.

The 1914 Mormon Tabernacle is among a number of striking early-20th-century structures.

THE SPRING CITY TABERNACLE

The Mormons

The official name is The Church of Jesus Christ of Latter Day Saints, but they are better known as Mormons. The sect has its origins in Fayette, New York, where, in 1830, Joseph Smith, Jr., the son of a New England farmer, published his revelations. Called *The Book of Mormon*, it traced the lost tribes of Israel to America centuries before the birth of Christ. The religion's most controversial tenant was its support of polygamy, because it was practiced by the biblical patriarchs. In 1831 Smith led a group of about 70 followers west to Ohio; in 1839, they moved again, this time to Nauvoo, Illinois. There, while Smith was in jail for destroying the offices and equipment of a rival Mormon sect's newspaper, he was murdered by an irate mob of Illinois militiamen. His successor was a carpenter and an elder of the church, Brigham Young, who was determined to lead his people West where they could finally escape persecution. In July 1847, after an arduous journey, he reached his destination - the Great Salt Lake Basin, an arid wasteland that Young reasoned no one else would want. Through a system of dams and irrigation ditches, the Mormons turned the inhospitable environment into an oasis that they called the State of Deseret. Its capital, Salt Lake City, was an impressive, well-planned community with a towering temple as its centerpiece (completed in 1893). In 1850, Deseret became the Territory of Utah, with Young as its first Governor. Following a dispute with President James Buchanan in 1857, the Mormon leader was removed from office. When an armed clash ensued between the Morman militia and the U.S. army, the Mormons lost control of the Territory. In 1890, they agreed to abandon polygamy and six years later Utah entered the Union as the 45th state.

BRIGHAM YOUNG

From the Virginia City cemetery, one can look past the mine dumps to the boisterous town where silver flowed as freely as whiskey.

(*Opposite*) The Piper Opera House, played host to many of the great entertainers who toured the West during the later portion of the 19th century. Its antique scenery and props are still used in local theatrical productions.

A million dollars in a single month? Such a fabulous take was not unusual during the boom years of the Comstock Lode in northwestern Nevada, the richest silver deposit ever discovered in the United States—which also was 45 percent gold. At the peak, miners worked 365 days a year at seven major mine sites along the 2½-mile-long deposit extending northward from Gold Canyon.

The effects of such riches—the value ultimately exceeded $400 million dollars—were predictable in the heady atmosphere of the 19th-century American West. Nevada was transformed in less than five years from an ignored and underpopulated section of Utah Territory into first a separate territory and then, in 1864, a state. As author Robert Laxalt has said, "Virginia City is where Nevada really began."

Virginia City sprang up in 1859 near the site where two prospectors discovered gold and where prospector Henry Tompkins Paige Comstock conned them into a partnership by convincing them he owned the land. The town got its name from a ne'er-do-well nicknamed "Old Virginny," who christened the site with a bottle he had dropped because he didn't want it to go to waste. Virginia City quickly became the Queen of the Comstock, the largest and most boisterous of the 24-hour-a-day mining towns of the region. It remained,

Before he worked in Virginia City as a newspaper reporter, Mark Twain tried his hand at prospecting. His experiences in the West provided useful material for several of his books.

through the 1860s and into the late 1870s, the center of the most productive mining district in the world. In 1875, a fire destroyed 33 square blocks of homes and commercial buildings, but the town recovered within a year and became the most important community between San Francisco and Denver, with more than 10,000 inhabitants.

Like most mining towns, Virginia City had a multiple personality. The miners, who worked hard and risked cave-ins, fires, and occasional flooding, indulged in a perpetual party during their leisure hours. Gambling and drinking went on night and day; as much as $6,000 might change hands at a single sitting and quarrels sometimes ended in fistfights or gunfights. This

atmosphere provided lively material for the imaginative minds of people like Mark Twain, who got his start as a reporter for the *Territorial Enterprise* in Virginia City.

Virginia City's renaissance as a tourist center, which began in the 1950s, has produced a lively town. The main street, which has the unpretentious name of C Street, is flanked by scores of historic structures housing modern businesses, many of them resplendent in bright paint. Descendants of famous saloons, where fortunes were won or lost in a card game, include Sundance, Red Garter, and Delta, as well as the Old Washoe Club. An exterior plaque notes that today's Silver Queen Saloon was originally Molinelli's

The One-Room Schoolhouse

Book learning was cherished in the Old West. Even though the taming of the wilderness was difficult work, most new towns sought to provide some form of schooling for their youths. Many had to make do with a one-room structure, in which all of the grades were ensconced together on a row-by-row basis. The one-room school near Crede, Colorado, had almost 80 students in 1892! Public schools were often established with funds derived from the sale of

federally-owned land, given to new territories by Congress in order to encourage education. Erecting a building was relatively easy; finding qualified teachers was hard. It wasn't a very lucrative job. One could earn no more than about $35 a month, and that would only be paid during the five months or so when school was in session. Room and board would typically be provided too, with teachers living on a rotating basis with the families of their pupils; those with the largest number of youngsters would be obliged to house the teacher for the longest period of time. If a professional couldn't be found, sometimes an educated greenhorn, a new arrival in town, would be impressed into the job. Most of the teachers were women; often they were barely older than their students and more often than not, they saw teaching as a temporary stop-gap before marriage. As for the schooling itself, recitation, memorization, and copying accounted for most of the work.

A SCHOOLROOM IN VIRGINIA CITY'S FOURTH WARD.

Hotel, which operated from 1875 until the 1940s, and that a fudge parlor began as the hall for the Odd Fellows, an organization that was strong throughout the Western goldfields.

The covered wooden sidewalks of the community once again teem with motion and excitement as tourists re-capture some of the ambience of the Comstock era. A 15-minute audiovisual program at the Visitors Center in the heart of the historical area prepares tourists for the highly commercialized version of a 19th-century goldfield town. Visitors may descend old shafts of the Best and Belcher or Chollar mines to learn about stopes, drifts, crosscuts, raises, and winzes or ride the Virginia & Truckee Railroad over a few miles of 1869 track between Vir-ginia City and Gold Hill, another Gold Rush community. They may attend performances at Piper Opera House, still furnished with the scenery and props installed in the 1880s, when pa-trons pelted their favorite performers with gold coins. They may view numerous mining artifacts at The Way It Was and Wild West Museums or take in the wonders of the Mark Twain Museum of Memories, which include 19th-century costumes, Indian and mining artifacts, and a mannequin that recites excerpts from the works of Samuel Clemens. They also may watch ungainly camels race, a reminder that the animals were used to haul freight to gold camps.

Away from this tourist core a calmer atmosphere prevails. The 1860 Mac-Kay House, a 10-room mansion that initially housed the office of the Gould and Curry Mine, is now decorated with the furnishings of a subsequent resi-dent, John MacKay, an Irish immi-grant who rose to become one of the kings of the Comstock. An 1868 house named The Castle is filled with antique furnishings, including 200-year-old Czechoslovakian chandeliers, silver doorknobs, and marble fireplaces. Religious structures include the small, neat Presbyterian Church, the oldest in the town; St. Paul's Episcopal Church;

and St. Mary's in the Mountains Roman Catholic Church.

The otherwise rowdy miners prac-ticed a code of honor that prevented the harassment of women, and violators of the code were prosecuted. Further-more, the miners regularly contributed to worthy causes, especially those for the families of men lost in the mines. The deceased invariably received a

This impressive castle was built in 1863 by Robert Greaves, superin-tendant of the Empire Mine. It is filled with antique furnishings and sports doorknobs of silver.

(Following pages) Looking at these headstones, one can see that some people lived to fairly ripe old ages in this boisterous Nevada community.

good funeral, with a band leading the procession, regardless of his or her financial condition. Help was also extended to down-and-outers, who had staked all on a discovery and found nothing or those who had wasted their riches.

The wealthy in the community created their own lifestyle. New millionaires spent money freely to construct Victorian mansions and to lavishly fill them with stylish furniture. They imported delicacies such as oysters, caviar, and champagne for their parties and dances and financed the operation of luxurious hotels and restaurants. They also helped organize a lively social and cultural life centered around schools, churches, stores, and Piper's Opera House, which could afford to bring in the greatest stage celebrities of the period—Sarah Bernhardt, Lillian Russell, and Lotta Crabtree among them. President Ulysses S. Grant and his family stopped in Virginia City during his around-the-world tour after leaving office. His Civil War comrades Generals William Tecumseh Sherman and Philip Sheridan, as well as President Rutherford B. Hayes, also received warm welcomes. It was not unusual for visitors to put on miner's suits and descend some 4,000 feet into the mines.

In 1877, the Comstock Lode began to play out and the demonetization of silver by Congress accelerated Virginia City's downfall. One by one, the great mines and mills closed down and the miners moved on, many heading for new gold discoveries. The millionaires hurried to San Francisco and other amenable cities, where they could continue to indulge themselves. By 1900, the Queen of the Comstock was a shabby shadow, inhabited by a few thousand hangers-on.

The Miners Union Hall, built in 1876, was the headquarters of the first labor organization for miners in the United States, the Fraternal Order of Eagles.

(Opposite) This neat frame Presbyterian Church is the oldest religious building in the town.

THE FIREHOUSE

EST. 1853

1112

This Front Street advertisement for the California Steam Navigation Company reminds visitors to present-day Sacramento of the role that river traffic played in the founding and early development of the town

(*Opposite*) A setting sun casts shadows across the facade of the 1853 firehouse, one of the oldest extant buildings in Sacramento. It is now a restauranrt.

"The advantages which this sale now offers to merchants and mechanics wishing a residence near the mines, are too evident for comment," declared an advertisement in the December 23, 1848, issue of a San Francisco newspaper. Real estate promoters in mid-19th-century California were seldom that restrained, but any ad for lots in Sacramento would have done the job. A frenzied rush to the gold-bearing foothills of the Sierra Nevada Mountains had begun, following the accidental discovery of gold on the American River. Sacramento was strategically located to serve as a jumping off point for the hordes of Forty-Niners seeking mineral wealth.

The city was less than a year old when the ad appeared in the *California Star* and *Californian*. Located near the fort that pioneer John Augustus Sutter had built a few years earlier, it grew quickly as a transportation hub and supply center for the northern portion of the Mother Lode country. A tent city sprang up to service the prospectors moving through, but new arrivals lived wherever they could; some even slept in packing boxes and under trees. Ships were moored permanently as storehouses because space was not available ashore. Gradually, however, the tent city was replaced by more permanent structures, some of which remain today in historic Old Sacramento on the banks of the river.

The Railroad

At the outset of the 19th century, the nation's leaders expected that it would take 500 years to settle the West. Instead, the 1890 census declared the frontier closed. What made the difference, more than any other single factor, was the railroad. Spurred on by Congress and the state legislatures - which provided more than $64 million in bonds and 116 million acres in land grants - the railroad companies went from 3,200 miles of short-line track west of the Mississippi in 1865 to 72,000 miles by 1890. When the Railroad Act of 1862 called for the creation of a transcontinental railroad, the Union Pacific started west from Omaha, Nebraska, while the Central Pacific started east from Sacramento, California. Crossing two mountain chains - the Rockies and the Sierra Nevadas - and the Great

Basin, with its inadequate supplies of wood and water, they laid an average of two to five miles of track per day. On May 10, 1869, they met at Promontory Summit, Utah, and the nation was linked by rail. During the ensuing year, 150,000 passengers made the journey between Omaha and Sacramento. A decade later, the figure

THE SACRAMENTO RAILROAD STATION (left) AND WAITING ROOM (above)

approached 1 million. "A journey over the plains was a formidable undertaking, requiring great patience and endurance," reported *Frank Leslie's Illustrated Newspaper.* "Now all that has changed. . . the six months' journey is reduced to less than a week." And thus the way for people to come West had been eased, and the heavy flow of goods between the frontier and the rest of the nation had begun.

Almost from the start, the city began building a permanent economic base for the inevitable day when gold mining would decline. Sutter had proved, before the Gold Rush decimated his herds and trampled his fields, that agriculture could thrive in the central valley around the town. When discouraged miners began returning from the goldfields, some turned to farming or their former trades, creating industries such as carriage shops, breweries, canning plants, and farm machinery factories.

By 1850, Sacramento numbered 6,820 residents; it had at least 10,000 shortly thereafter. Indeed, nothing seemed to inhibit the growth of the city. A cholera epidemic in 1850, which caused three-fourths of the residents to flee and killed hundreds of people, was only a temporary setback. So were disastrous floods in 1850 and 1853 and a fire in 1852, which wiped out two-thirds of the town.

Sacramentans pursued urban achievement with a fever that rivaled their lust for gold. In 1849, they offered the state legislature $1 million to select their city as the state capital; a year later, it was so designated. Transportation flourished after 1860 when the Pony Express established its western terminus there. In 1869, the first transcontinental railroad trains began rolling in, transferring passengers to riverboats bound for San Francisco, where those who wished to could board ships for the eastern United States and other parts of the world.

Today's Sacramento reflects many aspects of its historic past. The largest and most striking relic is Old Sacramento, whose original and reconstructed buildings, board sidewalks, and cobblestone streets recall the Gold Rush period. The 28-acre restoration, which began in 1965, includes 44 buildings that once housed banks, express offices, a newspaper, a firehouse, and other businesses. Some are made of red brick with tall, narrow windows; others are frame structures decorated with scrollwork.

Before the discovery of gold on his property in 1848, John Augustus Sutter had established a fort near Sacramento and created an agricultural settlement called New Helvetia.

The Union Hotel was popular with businessmen and politicians in the 1860s. It replaced the earlier Veranda Hotel, destroyed by fire in 1852.

A walking tour of Old Sacramento, starting at the Visitors Center in the California Steam Navigation Company Freight Depot on Front Street, pinpoints 19 structures, including the 1852 Lady Adams Building, the oldest original building in the old town section; the B. F. Hastings Building, raised soon after the fire of 1852, now housing a Communications Museum; and the reconstructed Eagle Theater, which opened in 1849 and is still the site of locally produced shows.

Sacramento's key role as the western terminus of the first transcontinental railroad is remembered by the California State Railroad Museum, which opened in 1981 and is the largest museum of its kind in the world. It has about 100 pieces of rolling stock and houses hundreds of relics in 40 interpretive displays. The reconstructed 1876 Central Pacific Passenger Station is an adjunct of the museum and a departure point for excursions.

Sacramento's rise was accompanied by the fall of the Sutter family. The agricultural colony founded by John Augustus Sutter had produced flour and lumber and, by 1848, had 4,000 cattle, 3,000 sheep, and 1,700 horses and mules. But after the discovery of gold it was inundated by a tide of prospectors who overran Sutter's fort, stole his cattle, drove off his Indian guards, and disputed his claim to the land. Sutter avoided the pressure of creditors by deeding his property to his son and opening a supply store at Coloma, where the discovery by James W. Marshall had initiated the Gold Rush. Laying out the town of Sacramento was part of the effort of John Sutter, Jr., to alleviate his father's debt burden, but Sutter's fort had to be sold in 1849 to satisfy creditors. The senior Sutter took up residence at nearby Hock Farm with his family, newly arrived from Switzerland, while the question

This modern depot marks the western terminus of the Central Pacific Railroad, the last link in the nation's first transcontinental railway.

During the latter half of the 19th century, Sacramento's riverfront was a bustling place, as this vintage photograph illustrates. Today, the *Delta King* is a colorful reminder of that era. The paddlewheeler serves as a restaurant, bar, and convention center.

of his Mexican land grants moved slowly through the courts. In 1866, after his farmhouse burned, he moved to Washington, D.C., where he pressed Congress for compensation for his colonization work and the loss of his property. He died in 1880 at Lititz, Pennsylvania, without receiving it.

Sutter's original adobe and timber fort, which was cannibalized to obtain building materials during Sacramento's early days, was the object of one of the nation's first historical conservation efforts. In 1890, the Central Building, virtually all that remained at the time, and a two-block site were acquired by public subscription and deeded to the state.

Now a state historic park, the reconstructed rectangular fort has walls 15 feet high and 2½ feet thick, with bastions at the northwest and southeast corners. The rooms within its walls are furnished to reflect the kind of life that existed at the fort in the 1840s when, according to poet Lucius Harwood Foote, "waifs of every clime, blown by the fickle winds of chance," visited the outpost. The Central Building has been restored to reflect its original uses, primarily as Sutter's office and residence.

The Dingley Spice and Coffee Mill stands near the Big Four Building, named after the men who founded the Central Pacific Railroad - Charles Crocker, Mark Hopkins, Collis Potter Huntington, and Leland Stanford.

The domed Nevada County Bank building, built in 1917, stands on Mill Street, the main route to the gold mines of Grass Valley.

(Opposite) Firehouse No. 2 in Nevada City was built in 1861 to house one of the city's first volunteer fire companies. The station is still in use.

"**E**ureka! I have found it!" was the universal cry of gold prospectors who hit paydirt. It echoed thousands of times in the rugged, wooded valleys of California's Sierra Nevada mountain range as crusty miners announced their new discoveries. In time, the exclamation was used to identify claims and even towns. It is still the motto of America's most populous state.

However, it may not be the most appropriate word to identify California's Gold Rush era because men *not* looking for gold had an uncanny way of finding it. At Grass Valley, for example, George McKnight is credited with the 1850 discovery of the rich quartz deposits which turned the Gold Rush into a long-lasting bonanza. According to the legend, he stubbed a toe on a gold-impregnated rock while chasing a straying cow. The Empire Mine State Historical Park at Grass Valley tells its own version of events, crediting George Rogers, a lumberman, with the start of the region's mining era, when he spied flecks of gold in an outcropping of quartz rock.

Whoever did it, the area around Nevada City soon was pockmarked with "coyote holes," or 20- to 40-foot-deep wells into which miners were lowered in buckets. Such mining was arduous work, cave-ins were frequent, and the results were chancy. After the invention of hydraulic mining, individual

(Opposite) The Holbrook Hotel in Grass Valley is restored to its appearance in 1862, when it played host to Mark Twain, among others.

It is remarkable how much the Pine Street of Nevada City today resembles its 19th-century antecedent. Note the same dogleg in the street at the rear of both pictures where a highrise courthouse has taken the place of a smaller, classical structure.

claims were frequently consolidated into large tracts by companies that could afford to build miles of ditches for transporting the huge amounts of water necessary to support a successful mining operation. Similarly when quartz mining was developed, large amounts of money were necessary to underwrite stamp mills, cyanide tanks, and shafts needed to exploit the ore-bearing beds. Of course, those who succeeded found that the results more than compensated for the expenses. Indeed, the area produced more than half of California's total gold produc-

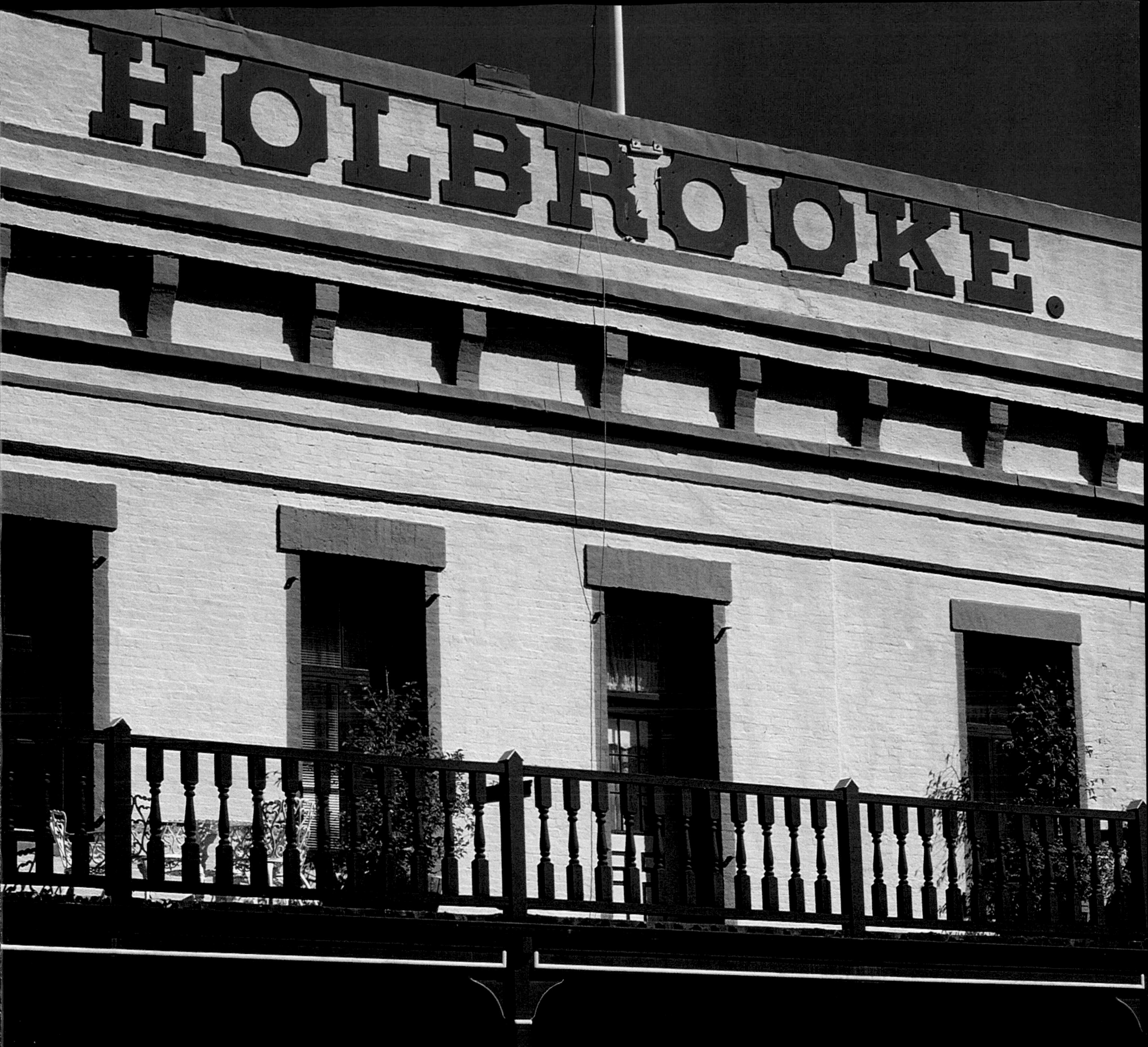
HOLBROOKE.

The Mines

When a rich vein of ore was discovered, a pick and a rocker were wholly inadequate to the task of tapping its depth. That required heavy machinery and manpower. Even if a prospector *had* the financial resources to launch such an enterprise, its stolid nature ran contrary, in most cases, to his adventuresome spirit. So more often than not a prospector sold his claim to those who stood ready to plummet the earth's hard core for riches. And plummet they did, reaching incline depths of as great as 11,100 feet (over 2 miles). There were several different methods for extracting the ore. One technique, known as hardrock min-

ing, called for blasting the rock, crushing it into a flour-like consistency and mixing it with water. The mixture was then washed across a table coated with mercury (which attracts gold) and the amalgam taken to a refinery where it was heated. As the temperature rose, the mercury evaporated, leaving the gold. The residue was then taken to another furnace, where it was heated again, and poured into ingots. Another method for extracting ore was known as hydraulic mining. Through this technique, miners created a highly sophisticated version of a prospector's rocker, in which water carried to the shaft by a flume or a ditch - sometimes running 60 miles long or more - created pressure which separated the precious ore and sand from rock. The former then settled at the bottom of large trays, where the gold was separated from the sand by mercury. Sometimes in the pursuit of an adequate water source, mine owners would create dams at the tops of streams. One such structure broke and nearly destroyed the town of Marysville, California, in 1881. That event pretty much brought an end to hydraulic mining.

GRASS VALLEY'S EMPIRE MINE DURING ITS HEY-DAY (above) AND TODAY (left)

tion, or at least a billion dollars worth of ore.

Among the best-preserved survivors of the era are Grass Valley and Nevada City, each of which retains much of its flavor when lusty men and women from all areas of the world, including some free blacks who made fortunes in gold, staked out every inch of the adjoining countryside.

Grass Valley, once the richest gold mining town in California, was primarily a residential and commercial base for the nearby mines. Gold was everywhere; miners even dug up the town streets looking for it, on the theory that the law did not prevent them from doing so. In its heyday, it was also regarded as a choice homesite by the famous and near famous. Among the celebrities who settled there was actress-dancer Lola Montez, who lived in retirement in Grass Valley from 1852 to 1854 with a pet bear, some dogs, and a husband (whom she divorced after he killed the bear for clawing and biting him). The 1851 house where Lola lived is located on Mill Street, the town's main thoroughfare since 1849. Nearby is the two-story home of her protégée, Lotta Crabtree, who at the age of 16 scored triumphs in San Francisco and on the east coast and who remained a stage celebrity for 50 years.

Although many of Grass Valley's 300 frame buildings were destroyed by fire 100 years ago, a number of Gold Rush structures are among the 11 buildings in an eight-block walking tour. The restored Holbrook Hotel several blocks away on West Main Street provides insight into the kind of Gold Rush accommodations experienced by Mark Twain and others. The Union Square Building on Mill Street was home for 76 years to the town's newspaper, founded in 1864. The North Star Mining Museum, on Alli-

(*Opposite*) The Nevada City Miners Foundry, built in 1865, houses a museum that focuses on the decorative arts of the Victorian age. It also hosts an annual teddy bear convention.

The handsome Emmanuel Episcopal Church in Grass Valley was established in 1858. It is the oldest Episcopal church in the region.

son Branch Road, displays mining equipment, including a 30-foot Pelton Wheel, a famous device which helped bridge the gap between the waterwheel and modern generators.

Empire Mine, on Ophir Hill one mile south of Grass Valley, opened in 1850, changed hands often, and was considerably altered by successive groups of owners. Shafts eventually reached 7,000 feet below the surface and had more than 365 miles of passageways. Over the course of its boom-and-bust history, which lasted until 1956, the mine produced nearly 6 million ounces of gold worth more than $100 million. Now part of a 788-acre state park, the complex exhibits more than a dozen structures and the ruins of a few others, dating from 1896 to 1929. Among them are the Empire Cottage, built in 1898, where the owners lived when on the site; and the combination assay office and retort room, where amalgam from the stamp mill was reduced to a partially refined gold "sponge" for shipment to government mints. Displays in the Visitors Center depict the hazards associated with mining, the processes used at the mine, and the contributions of immigrant miners.

Nevada City, 4 miles away from Grass Valley, traces its roots to a discovery by James W. Marshall at Deer Creek in the summer of 1848. Within two years, 10,000 miners worked claim to claim within a radius of 3 miles, some able to pan a pound of gold a day. The seat of Nevada County progressed through the various stages of gold mining: placer diggings in the 1850s and 1860s, hydraulic excavations of the 1870s, and deep-shaft quartz mining from the 1880s through the early decades of the 20th century.

Nevada City was not only rich, it was lucky. Many handsome brick business buildings escaped seven disastrous fires. And, as gold mining declined, the town became a haven for many wealthy families from San Francisco. It was among the first towns to convert historic factories and stores into chic

This home in Grass Valley resembles an English country manor. It was one of several residences built in the 19th century by Empire Mine owner William Bourne.

restaurants, museums, antique stores, and theaters. Consequently, it is one of the best-preserved mining towns in northern California and rates a place on the National Register of Historic Places.

A walking tour highlights 11 old buildings conveniently located on four streets. Historic Broad Street structures include the Old Nevada Theatre, which opened in July 1865 and was reopened after restoration 100 years later; and the three-story National Hotel, in operation since 1856. Each is the oldest continuously operating facility of its kind in California. Three historic structures are near the 1855 South Yuba Canal Building, now occupied by the Chamber of Commerce: the assay office, which tested the first samples from Nevada's fabulous Comstock Lode; J. J. Jackson's general store, which provisioned many a Gold Rush miner; and Firehouse No. 1, which houses the Nevada County Historical Museum.

Fourteen miles from Nevada City is Malakoff Diggins State Historic Park, whose 3,000 acres also provide major outdoor recreational activities. It was the site of the world's largest hydraulic gold mine before California banned such mining in 1884 through one of the nation's first environmental laws. Structures and exhibits there explore the lifestyles of the 1870s and the use of pressurized jets of water to obtain ore.

Retired actress-dancer Lola Montez lived for two years in an 1851 house in Grass Valley where she helped coach teenager Lotta Crabtree for stardom.

The World Museum of Mining and
Hell-Roarin' Gulch in Butte, Montana

Acknowledgments

The producers of *Legendary Towns of the Old West* gratefully acknowledge the following individuals who assisted in the creation of this book:

Alaska State Library, Gladi Kulp, Kay Shelton, India Spartz; Arizona Historical Society, Lori Davisson, Deborah Sehlton; Arizona State Library & Archives, Carol Downey; Auburn Chamber of Commerce, Marianne Kollenberg; Barker-Texas Archives, The University of Texas at Austin, John Slate; Boise Basin Museum, Johnny Thompson; Boot Hill Museum, Fay Trent, Darleen Clifton Smith; Butte Archives, Ellen Crain; Butte Chamber of Commerce, Maureen Roche; California State Library, John Gonzales, Carol Gilbert, Gary Kurutz, Rhonda Fisher; Peggy Calloway; Church of Jesus Christ of Latter Day Saints, Bryan Sokolowsky; Colorado Historical Society, Rebecca Lintz; Columbia State Historic Park, George Speaker; Joy Comstock; Deadwood Chamber of Commerce, Laurie Heinen, Tom Stuart; Deadwood Public Library, Terri Davis, Margaret Pontius; Dedman's Photo Shop (Skagway, Alaska), Barbera Kalen; Denver Public Library, Kathey Swan; Department of Parks and Recreation, Sacramento District Historic Sites, Nancy Mendez; Durango Chamber of Commerce, Kristen Plese; El Pueblo De Los Angeles Park, Tina Stern; Empire Mine State Park, Evelyn Whisman, Jim Burke; Estes Park Historical Society, Mel Busch, Linda Vogel; Firehouse Museum, Francis Jones, Catherine Citizen; Fredericksburg, Texas Chamber of Commerce, Joe Kammlah; Georgetown, Colorado Chamber of Commerce, Kay Parker; Golden Spike Empire Travel Region, Connie Flinders; Grass Valley Chamber of Commerce, Carole Peters; Guthrie Chamber of Commerce, Jane Thomas; Harrison House (Guthrie, Oklahoma), Phyllis Murray and staff; Helena, Montana Historical Society, Pat Bick; Historic Preservation Commission, Spring City, Utah, Kaye Watson; Historical Santa Fe Foundation, Marianna Anders; Idaho State Historical Society, Guila Ford, Larry Jones, Elizabeth Jacox; Institute of Texan Cultures, Tom Shelton; Kansas Heritage Center, Jeannie Covalt; Kansas State Historical Society, Christie Stanley; Klondike Gold Rush National Historical Park, Clay Alrickson; Leadville Chamber of Commerce, Nikki Shilds, Valerie Mondragon; Lincoln County Heritage Trust, Bob Hart, Gary Miller; Mansfield Library, University of Montana, Dale Johnson; Marshall Gold Discovery Park, Connie Price; Montana Historical Society; Museum of New Mexico, Orlando Romero, Arthur Olivas; Nevada City Chamber of Commerce, Kathy Whittlesey; Nevada Historical Society, Phillip Earl, Erik Lauritzen; North Dakota Historical Society, Mel Barnett; Oklahoma Historical Society, Kay Zahrai, Robert Nespor; Old Sacramento Historic District, Lynn Hanson, Lucy Steffens; Old Town Association, Albuquerque, Marie Valient; Rosenberg Library, Casey Greene; Searls Historical Library, Edwin Tyson; Sharlot Hall Museum, Prescott, Arizona, Sue Abbey; Silverton Chamber of Commerce, Rich Olsen; Southern Oregon Historical Society, Sue Waldron, Carol Harbison; State of Oklahoma, Tourism and Recreation Department, Lisa Harp Austerman; Taos Pueblo, Vera Lefthand, Elaine Romero; Telluride Chamber of Commerce, Paul Campbell; Territorial Musuem, Guthrie, Oklahoma, Mike Bruce; Texas State Library, John Anderson, Dave Richards; The Copper King Mansion, Ann Cote Smith; The Stuhr Museum of the Prairie Pioneer, Tom Anderson; The University of Oklahoma, John Lovett, Elizabeth Mobley; Tombstone, Chamber of Commerce, Jim Lindsey; Robert Torrez; Ben Traywick; University of Wyoming, James Carlson; Utah Historical Society, Gary Topping, Susan Whetstone, Roger Ropper, Dave Shyer; Virginia City (Montana) Chamber of Commerce, Bruce McCallum; Virginia City (Nevada) Historical Society, Eric Moody; Kay Watson; Wells Fargo Bank/History Department, Robert Chandler; World Musuem of Mining, Allan Hooper; Wyoming Historical Society, Mark Junge; Wyoming State Archives, Ann Nelson, Paula Chavoya.

Photo Credits

All of the color photographs in this volume are courtesy of Lynn Radeka, except for the images of Skagway, Alaska, which were taken by Lewis Kemper. The historic photographs were supplied by the following sources:

Alaska State Library 99, 103; American Heritage Center, University of Wyoming 31, 150; Arizona Historical Society 139; Boot Hill Museum, Inc., Dodge City, Ks. 19, 49, 142; California State Library, California Section 163, 166, 172, 175; Centennial Archives, Deadwood Public Library 34; Church of Jesus Christ of Latter Day Saints 151; Colorado Historical Society 48; Denver Public Library, Western History Department 38, 39, 54; Historic Preservation Committee, Spring City, Utah 149; Idaho State Historical Society 84; Library of Congress 15, 60; Lincoln County Heritage Trust 130; VM Mansfield Library, University of Montana 79; Montana Historical Society 71; Museum of New Mexico 125, 127, 130, 133; Nevada Historical Society 4, 154; Oklahoma Historical Society 114; Rosenberg Library, Galveston, Texas 109; Searls Historical Library 170; Southern Oregon Historical Society 90, 93, 95; SuperStock 23; Wells Fargo Bank 64; Western History Collections, University of Oklahoma 119; World Museum of Mining 74; Wyoming State Archives, Museums, and Historical Department 30.